THE BEST OF
OLYMPIC
NATIONAL PARK

by ALAN LEFTRIDGE

D1496531

ACKNOWLEDGMENTS

Thank you Linda, for sharing and co-contributing the content of this book. Jenny Baker and LK Duvanich contributed several quality photographs. Thanks to Jim Covel and Christine Revelas for their suggestions about marine life of the Pacific Northwest. I also want to acknowledge Will Harmon, Farcountry Press editor, for his championing of the "Best of [National Parks]" series and interpretive writing techniques. Finally, I want to express my appreciation to the volunteers and park service staff at Olympic for sharing with me their knowledge, affection, and enthusiasm for this magnificent national park.

ISBN: 978-1-56037-643-9

© 2016 by Farcountry Press
Text and photography © 2016 by Alan Leftridge except where noted otherwise

Cover photograph © Floris van Breugel
Inset cover photographs by Alan Leftridge and the National Park Service

All rights reserved. This book may not be reproduced in whole or in part by any means (with the exception of short quotes for the purpose of review) without the permission of the publisher.

For more information about our books, write Farcountry Press, P.O. Box 5630, Helena, MT 59604; call (800) 821-3874; or visit www.farcountrypress.com.

Cataloging-in-Publication data on file at the Library of Congress.

 Produced and printed in the United States of America.

24   23   22   21   20   2   3   4   5   6   7

PREFACE

I am visiting Olympic for the first time, what is there to see and do? This is a question that you might ask a park employee or a friend familiar with the park. But you may have neither person to ask as you arrange your vacation. Since you have limited time to tour the park, it is best to plan your visit so that you can enjoy Olympic's best sites and activities.

The purpose of this book is to enhance your visit by sharing the natural history and cultural heritage of Olympic National Park. I will relate to you the iconic features—the best of the park—as identified by people who know the park. This book shares with you what I think you should know about Olympic as if you were a family member or friend visiting for the first time.

I encourage you to experience new connections with the land. I want you to recognize some of the adaptations that plants and animals have for living in this wild, untamed place. I'll also give you ideas about how to best share your experiences with family and friends.

This book is meant to inspire you to experience the adaptive diversity and the abundance of life in Olympic National Park. I encourage you to follow your interests in exploring, hiking, photographing, viewing wildlife and wildflowers, and learning about the park's natural and cultural history. The experiences that you have and the stories that you build will lead you to the essence of Olympic National Park.

Alan Leftridge

HOW TO USE THE MAPS IN THIS BOOK

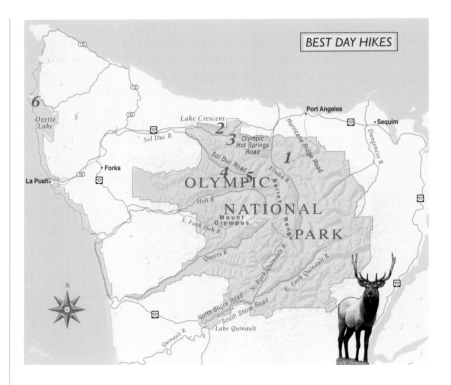

The maps in this book show numbered locations for features and activities described in each chapter. Some indicate general areas, while others show more specific locations for individual subjects explained in the text. Use these maps with the more detailed visitor map you receive at any entrance station. For hiking, backpacking, and climbing, more detailed topographic maps are recommended, available at vendors in communities around the park.

OLYMPIC'S LEGACY

You may have already experienced the delicate wonders of a rain-soaked forest or clambered over wave-tossed driftwood giants on an endless wild beach. Perhaps you have marveled at the rising sun burnishing the Olympic Mountains in radiant splendor. Olympic National Park is a special place that offers opportunities for a range of peak experiences.

Because of the myriad opportunities for enjoyment, Olympic National Park claims a high rate of return visitors. Generations of people have gathered in the park seeking experiences, building memories, and sharing their stories with loved ones. The dynamic geography and unique ecosystems, preserved by progressive-minded people, allow us to immerse ourselves in the wonders of the natural world. The discoveries you make and memories you build with your families and friends will span lifetimes. This is the legacy of Olympic.

WHERE IS OLYMPIC NATIONAL PARK?

Look at your copy of the official park map. Notice that the park is but a part of the Olympic Peninsula. The rest of the peninsula is tribal land, national forest holdings, and private property.

During the Pleistocene, a glacier 1 mile thick surrounded the Olympic Mountains. When the ice receded, it left the waters of Puget Sound and Hood Canal to the east, and the Strait of Juan de Fuca to the north, isolating a peninsula from the mainland.

This geophysical separation isolated plant and animal populations, leading to higher than expected numbers of species that are native only to the peninsula. Five mammals, five insects, three fish, two mollusks, one amphibian, and eight plants are endemic to the Olympic Peninsula. The park's biotic uniqueness reflects its climatic diversity. The unique topography of the landscape also fosters prodigious precipitation, in turn growing some of the world's largest trees.

Early explorers of the peninsula voiced the need for preservation of the unique environment. Congress agreed, and 922,651 acres of the most representative features of the peninsula are preserved in Olympic National Park.

OLYMPIC: JUST THE FACTS

- President Theodore Roosevelt created Mount Olympus National Monument on March 2, 1909. His fifth cousin, President Franklin Roosevelt, designated it as a national park on June 29, 1938.

- Olympic National Park is 922,651 acres (1,442 square miles), more than 10 times the size of Seattle.

- It is the largest intact primeval rain forest in the contiguous 48 states.

- Olympic is the 13th largest of the 59 designated national parks.

- Ninety-five percent of the park is managed as wilderness.

- The highest peak in the park is Mount Olympus at 7,980 feet above sea level.

- The park has 73 miles of undeveloped coastline, the longest undeveloped coast in the contiguous United States.

- Eleven river systems drain the Olympic Mountains.

- The park receives over 3 million visits per year; most people are from the state of Washington.

- There are 60 named glaciers in the Olympic Mountains.

- The park has 611 miles of maintained trails.

- Between 12 to 14 feet of rainfall can occur annually.

- The largest wild herd of Roosevelt elk lives here.

- There are 32 terrestrial mammal species found in Olympic National Park.

- The waters of Olympic National Park are home to 37 native aquatic species.

- There are 24 marine mammal species.

- More than 250 bird species occur in the park.

PLAN YOUR VISIT

Every national park has its must-see features. For Yellowstone, it is Old Faithful; Yosemite, Half Dome and the valley; Glacier has the Going-to-the-Sun Road; and the Grand Canyon . . . well you get the idea. If you have but one day to visit Olympic, make sure that you explore Hurricane Ridge. Of course, there are myriad other outstanding things to see and do in the park, so here are my suggestions on how to plan your visit, in one-day excursions:

Learn about the natural and cultural heritage of Olympic National Park by experiencing these iconic places.

- Stop at the Olympic National Park Visitor Center for an overview of the park features.

- Drive to Hurricane Ridge and marvel at the peaks and glaciers of the Olympic Mountains. The park is dominated by the mountains, but this is one of the few places you will see their expanse.

- Visit the Hurricane Ridge Visitor Center.

- Stroll the subalpine meadows on the Meadow Loop Trail.

- Explore the Lake Crescent area and hike to Marymere Falls.

President Grover Cleveland designated the park area as Olympic Forest Reserve in 1897 to preserve the exceptional primeval trees within. Experience why a president was so moved by trees; spend a day exploring the forests.

- Hike through a lowland forest to Sol Duc Falls (then visit Sol Duc Hot Springs Resort).

- Drive to the Hoh Rain Forest and walk the Trail of Mosses Nature Trail.

- Explore the Quinault Rain Forest and complete the Quinault River Drive.

- See the Queets River corridor to watch water from Mount Olympus rushing to the sea.

- Stroll Kalaloch Beach and Ruby Beach for the ocean environments and the coastline forests.

Offshore is the Flattery Rocks National Wildlife Refuge and Wilderness, protecting the park's beaches and tide pools. Explore these wild beach environments.

- La Push (First, Second, and Third Beaches).
- Rialto Beach, walk to see Hole-in-the-Wall.
- Shi Shi Beach, for its wide stretches of sand, tide pools, and sea stacks.
- Ozette Lake, remote, serene, and close to the beach.

There is so much more to see.

- Glines Canyon Dam removal site on the Elwha River. Restoration at its best.
- Deer Park Road and the Rain Shadow Nature Trail on Blue Mountain. The panoramas are fantastic.
- Explore old Douglas-fir forests along the North Fork Skokomish River in the Staircase area.

You will do a lot of driving. Olympic is a huge park with some roads working their way toward the interior to special features, but none crossing the Olympic Mountains. So you will likely backtrack often. Make sure to bring the following on your travels:

— Food and drinks; there are few options for supplies once you leave Port Angeles or Forks.

— Rain gear. Make sure it's heavy duty. Lightweight ponchos are not recommended.

— Layered clothing; temperatures can fluctuate widely in a short time.

— Extra clothing, in case you need to change into something dry.

— Waterproof (or a change of) shoes.

— Extra socks

— A warm hat

- — Sunglasses
- — Sunscreen
- — Lip balm
- — Hiking/walking shoes
- — A daypack
- — Camera
- — Field guides
- — Maps
- — Binoculars
- — Cooler with food and drinks

Marymere Falls Trail, Alan Leftridge

WEATHER AND CLIMATE

Weather is the transitory condition of the atmosphere—the ever-changing temperature, humidity, sunshine, wind, and rain. Climate is the overall pattern of weather averaged over a long time.

Olympic National Park's large and exceptionally diverse landscape means that weather is often different from one location to the next. The coast may be sunny at the same time that the mountaintops are obscured by clouds. You might leave a steady downpour in the rain forest to find it clear and breezy on Hurricane Ridge. The weather can be unpredictable and subject to rapid changes.

Olympic's climate is more foreseeable. Olympic has a moderate maritime climate with temperate summers and cool, mild winters. Summers are fair and warm, with average daytime highs between 65 and 75 degrees F and lows in the 50s. Summer is also the driest season.

The winter climate is mild, with temperatures in the 30s and 40s at lower elevations. Higher in the mountains, below freezing temperatures are common, but the mercury seldom dips below zero.

Rainfall, on average, is between 12 to 14 feet on the west side of the park, making it the wettest place in the contiguous United States. Fewer than 10 miles away, that rain becomes winter snow in the alpine zone, with accumulations of 10 feet. Another 10 miles east of the Olympic Mountains a rain shadow is formed, making it one of the driest areas on the north coast.

Olympic's weather may be variable, but the climate is more stable. Whatever the forecast, you should be prepared for wet conditions. Layer your clothing, bring rain gear and waterproof shoes, and keep a dry change of clothes handy.

TEN THINGS YOU MAY NOT KNOW ABOUT OLYMPIC

- One name first suggested for Olympic National Park was Elk National Park, as it was intended to be a reserve for dwindling elk herds.

- Hurricane Ridge is the westernmost ski area in the contiguous United States.

- Olympic National Park has no venomous snakes.

- Park headquarters is outside the park; it was the first park headquarters to be situated outside of its park.

- The park has 60 named glaciers, making it the third-largest glacier system in the 48 states.

- There are more than 650 archaeological sites in the park.

- Olympic National Park is a World Heritage Site and an International Biosphere Reserve.

- Four presidents have helped to preserve the lands of and around Olympic National Park: Grover Cleveland in 1897 designated the Olympic Forest Reserve, in 1909 Theodore Roosevelt established Mount Olympus National Monument, Franklin Roosevelt signed the Olympic National Park Act in 1938, and Harry Truman in 1953 added the Queets River Valley to the park.

- The park registers over 3 million visits annually; most visitors are Washington state residents.

- Olympic National Park is the wettest place in the contiguous United States.

A SHORT CULTURAL HISTORY OF OLYMPIC

Hoh ocean canoe, NOAA photo

The Olympic Peninsula's abundant and diverse natural resources have sustained human habitation for at least 12,000 years. Early Native Americans discovered ample hunting, fishing, and gathering resources that provided all of their food needs. Pristine water and abundant shelter opportunities allowed them to stay and thrive. Little changed over the millennia, and few traces of their impacts on the environment remain. Contact with ships and Euro-American settlers brought disease and cultural and environmental changes that were irrevocable.

Settlers brought their own ways of survival and imposed them upon the land. Farmers cleared land for crops, hunters reduced game populations, and logging changed forest composition on the peninsula. The establishment of Olympic National Park is a story of the preservation of an extraordinary natural environment.

Outside attention had been drawn to the peninsula by early settlers. Expeditions were mounted by the U.S. Army and the *Seattle Press* newspaper to explore the rugged, undeveloped interior. The exploration prompted Lieutenant Joseph O'Neil to write in his 1890 report, "I would state that while the country on the outer slope of these mountains is valuable, the interior is useless for all practicable purposes. It would, however, serve admirably for a national park."

Clear-cut hillsides brought opposition to rampant logging by the late 1800s. President Cleveland, saving much of the peninsula's remaining forested land, designated the Olympic Forest Reserve in 1897. His action preserved the balance of this magnificent ecosystem.

President Theodore Roosevelt, focusing more on wildlife, created Mount Olympus National Monument in 1909, primarily to protect the subalpine calving grounds and summer range of the native elk.

Civic debate over logging increased in the 1920s as tourists were exposed to the destructive harvesting methods. Public desire for preservation of some of the peninsula as Lieutenant O'Neil envisioned grew until President Franklin Roosevelt established Olympic National Park in 1938.

BEST HISTORIC SITES

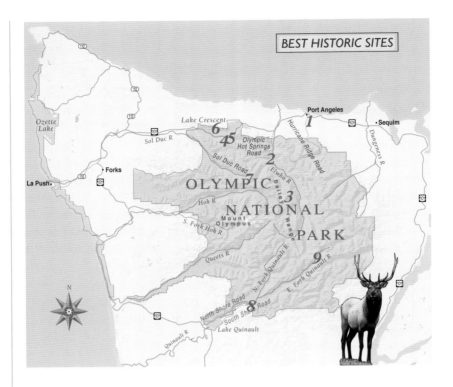

The National Register of Historic Places lists 28 properties and districts in Olympic National Park. They include rustic shelters, fire lookouts, ranger stations, guard stations, cabins, lodges, homesteads, chalets, and even a communal kitchen. The following are some of the most interesting historic places that you can reach easily by foot or vehicle.

1. Olympic National Park Visitor Center

Although it is situated just outside the park in Port Angeles, the visitor center is worthy of being one of the best historic sites. It was constructed, along with several other buildings, in 1940 and 1941 by the Public Works Administration with help from the Civilian Conservation Corps. Tour the visitor center to get a feel for the unique National Park Service rustic architecture.

2. Glines Canyon Dam Site

Glines Canyon Dam was built on the Elwha River in 1927. It was privately funded and, along with its companion, Elwha Dam, was constructed to provide electricity to the Port Angeles area. Both dams became obsolete and were removed. The Elwha Dam, which was outside

the park, was removed in 2012, and the Glines Canyon Dam was partially removed in 2013. Today, you can visit this site on Olympic Hot Springs Road and walk along the top of the dam over the spillway, and to the breach where the Elwha River flows freely after a century of impoundment. Interpretive displays tell the

Glines Canyon Dam, Alan Leftridge

stories of the construction of the dam, its impact on the environment, the dam's removal, and the restoration of the watershed.

3. Dodger Point Fire Lookout

The U.S. Forest Service built the Dodger Point Fire Lookout in 1933 in what was then the Olympic National Forest. It became included in the park in 1938. Its location above treeline on Dodger Point made it an ideal location to spot fires, and to be one of the park's 13 Aircraft Warning Service stations during World War II. The National Register of Historic Places listed the lookout in 2007. A 14.1-mile trail leads to the lookout from the Whiskey Bend Trailhead off Olympic Hot Springs Road in the Elwha Valley.

4. Lake Crescent Lodge

Built in 1916, Lake Crescent Lodge was originally called Singer's Lake Crescent Tavern. The lodge is an ideal base camp for exploring the north-central area of the park. The lodge nestles amidst giant firs and hemlock trees on the shore of charming Lake Crescent. Accommodations feature cabins and lodge rooms with magnificent views of the lake.

Lake Crescent Lodge, Alan Leftridge

5. Storm King Ranger Station

The hike to Marymere Falls from Barnes Point starts at this ranger station along U.S. Highway 101 on the south shore of Lake Crescent. The U.S. Forest Service constructed the station in 1905, and it has been a ranger station since. Today, the station is staffed seasonally; you are welcome to visit.

Storm King Ranger Station, Alan Leftridge

6. Pyramid Peak Aircraft Warning Service Lookout

From 1942 to 1944, the U.S. Army staffed 13 Aircraft Warning Service stations in Olympic National Park. Employees of the National Park Service built some of the stations, including one atop 3,000-foot Pyramid Peak north of Lake Crescent. They were used to house observers who were to send alarms of enemy aircraft intrusions. The station was abandoned in June 1944 but remains as a historical artifact on the south side of the mountain. The lookout can be reached by trail from the Camp David Junior Road east of Fairholme. The National Register of Historic Places listed the lookout in 2007.

7. Canyon Creek Shelter

You will pass the Canyon Creek Shelter on your 0.8-mile hike to Sol Duc Falls. The Civilian Conservation Corps constructed the three-sided shelter in 1939. The CCC built two other shelters at Moose Lake and Hoh Lake. The Canyon Creek Shelter is the only shelter remaining and exemplifies the rustic style of park architecture.

8. Graves Creek Ranger Station

The Graves Creek Ranger Station was the first administrative building of Olympic National Park. The Civilian Conservation Corps built the station from 1939 to 1941 on Graves Creek. The station was more than one structure. The CCC built a residence, garage, and generator building. Built in the National Park Service rustic architectural style, all three structures make up a historic district and are listed on the National Register of Historic Places. From U.S. Highway 101 at Lake Quinault, follow the South Shore Road to Graves Creek Road and drive to the station at road's end.

9. Enchanted Valley Chalet

This rustic chalet near the East Fork of the Quinault River was built in 1931 for the Olympic Recreation Company. It was a favorite destination in the 1930s and 1940s. For a brief period during World War II, it was used as an Aircraft Warning Service station. It never regained its popularity as a vacation spot after the war. The building was restored in 1980 and again in 2010 and is now listed on the National Register of Historic Places. Today, it consists of a kitchen, dining room, and sleeping rooms. From the Graves Creek Ranger Station, the chalet is a 13.2-mile hike along the Quinault River.

CIVILIAN CONSERVATION CORPS IN OLYMPIC

One of President Franklin Roosevelt's first actions after taking office in 1933 was the formation of the Civilian Conservation Corps (CCC). Facing a nation in the depths of economic disaster, the president's mission was to help revive the country by employing thousands of young men to preserve America's natural and historical heritage. Teams of men, under the command of military personnel, were assigned projects to build the nation's rural infrastructure and reclaim despoiled landscapes. So urgent was the need to put men to work during the midst of the Great Depression, Congress passed the act and placed it on the president's desk in three days. It remained operational until 1942.

The first camp on the Olympic Peninsula was set up in 1933, thirty-eight miles west of Port Angeles. That camp was moved to the Elwha River, at the foot of Hurricane Ridge, in 1937. Projects that the CCC completed included the Elwha Ranger Station, Canyon Creek Shelter, Altair Campground Community Kitchen, and a ranger station on the Hoh River. They were charged with falling snags on the Sol Duc Burn, road construction, and planting trees. President Roosevelt reviewed their reforestation project during his tour in October 1937.

By 1940, another CCC camp was established near Lake Quinault. Participants constructed the Norwood Guard Station and the campground at Graves Creek.

The CCC assisted Works Progress Administration (WPA) and Public Works Administration (PWA) personnel to construct the park headquarters in 1939-1940. CCC members hauled stone from nearby Tumwater Creek quarry for the first floor of the building.

The CCC motto became "Passing the Legacy to Future Generations." You will find many elements of that legacy in Olympic National Park.

FOUR LEADERS WHO ADVOCATED FOR THE PARK

In 1938, Congress designated nearly a million acres on the Olympic Peninsula as part of the national park system, ensuring it would be protected unimpaired for future generations to enjoy. Among all the proponents, four individuals led the charge in advocating for a national park: President Franklin Roosevelt, Lieutenant Joseph O'Neil, Judge James Wickersham, and James Christie.

Franklin D. Roosevelt

Franklin D. Roosevelt, Library of Congress

Franklin Roosevelt's fifth cousin, Theodore Roosevelt, established Mount Olympus National Monument in 1909 through executive privilege of the Antiquities Act. For the next 30 years, legislation to convert the monument to national park status was continually defeated.

This changed when FDR visited the peninsula on October 1, 1937, wishing to influence public support for a park. The U.S. Forest Service, which saw its mandate as a duty to provide resource-based employment, hosted the president's trip. They purposely failed to invite National Park Service representatives. During the tour, Roosevelt's motorcade passed a heavily logged area, where Forest Service personnel had repositioned a sign advising that it was private land rather than federal. Upon seeing the ugly clear-cut, the president declared, "I hope the son-of-a-bitch who is responsible for this is roasting in hell." He learned that the Forest Service and their sign had deceived him. The trickery and destruction of federal land raised his fury, and he became more eager to convert the monument to park status.

During the next congressional session, Washington Congressman Monrad Wallgren introduced a bill to create a 634,000-acre park. The legislation gave Roosevelt the power to extend the park's boundaries. The bill passed, and the president signed the legislation on June 29, 1938, with Roosevelt adding another 187,000 acres to preserve the Elwha watershed and Hurricane Ridge.

Lieutenant Joseph P. O'Neil

U.S. Army Lieutenant O'Neil led two government-sponsored explorations of the Olympics. The 1885 expedition was the first to document the interior. It left Port Angeles for the high country, eventually reaching the Hurricane Ridge area.

Four years later, O'Neil commanded his soldiers and scientists along the North Fork Skokomish River and across to the Quinault River drainage. He was tasked with cutting a 5-foot-wide road over 93 miles, connecting the river systems. His group also surveyed the watersheds of nine river systems in the southern range.

Lieutenant O'Neil's 1890 official report closes with this comment: "I would state that while the country on the outer slope of these mountains is valuable, the interior is useless for all practicable purposes. It would, however, serve admirably for a national park." His vision was actualized 48 years later.

Judge James Wickersham (middle row, third from right), Library of Congress

Judge James Wickersham

Yosemite was about to become the second national park in 1890 when two well-known figures of the Seattle area had a chance encounter in the wilds of the Olympic forests. Lieutenant Joseph O'Neil and Judge James Wickersham met and discussed advocating for a national park when they were independently exploring the wilderness. Wickersham had influence with the publishing industry and access to U.S. Geological Survey director John Wesley Powell, the renowned explorer of the Grand Canyon. Through his writings to Powell and publishers, he proposed the creation of a park. The efforts of O'Neil and Wickersham were the first formal proposals for preservation. Wickersham relocated to Alaska and subsequently pushed for the creation of Mount McKinley (renamed Denali in 1980) National Park.

James Christie

Anticipating that Washington would soon become the 42nd state and troubled by the blank spot on the map, the *Seattle Press* newspaper advertised for "hardy citizens . . . to acquire fame by unveiling the mystery which wraps the land encircled by the snow capped Olympic range."

Outdoorsman and explorer James Christie volunteered to compose an expedition. Five others joined him and became known as the Press Party. Braving a harsh, snowy winter, they entered the Elwha Valley in late 1889 and for the next five months explored the Elwha and Quinault Valleys, reaching the coast in May 1890. You can still see Press Party trail blazes along the Elwha River trail in the park.

BEST VISITOR CENTERS

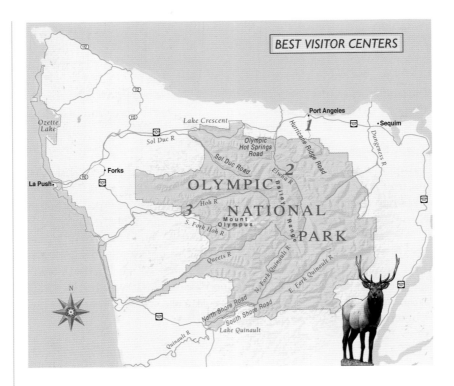

How will you know the best ways to manage your visit to Olympic? This book is meant to satisfy most of your questions, but speaking with a knowledgeable National Park Service employee or volunteer will enhance your experience. Familiarize yourself with the park by visiting its three visitor centers. Staff will report current roadway and trail conditions, point you in the direction of facilities, and share how to best explore the park.

1. Olympic National Park Visitor Center

The Olympic National Park Visitor Center is an essential stop before you venture along Hurricane Ridge Road. Park rangers and volunteers at the information desk will help you plan your

Olympic NP Visitor Center, Alan Leftridge

trip. Other resources available at the center are a children's Discovery Room, permanent exhibits, a bookshop, a theater featuring an orientation film, and nature trails out the back door.

2. Hurricane Ridge Visitor Center

For many people, this is their favorite visitor center in the park. When entering, you will see an information desk with at least one park ranger or volunteer ready to answer your questions. Exhibits here change annually. Whatever the weather, large windows provide views that change every moment. Around the corner from the information desk is the entrance to a small theater featuring an orientation film on the park. Venture downstairs and you will find a snack bar and a gift shop stocked with Northwest-oriented and Native American-themed items.

Hurricane Ridge Visitor Center, Alan Leftridge

3. Hoh Rain Forest Visitor Center

Do you have questions about the flora and fauna of the rain forest? This is a good place to find answers. Whether you talk with a volunteer or park ranger, the Hoh Rain Forest Visitor Center is a good place to tour. Be sure to explore the 0.8-mile Hall of Mosses Trail and 1.2-mile Spruce Nature Trail.

Hoh Rain Forest Visitor Center, Alan Leftridge

BEST LODGES

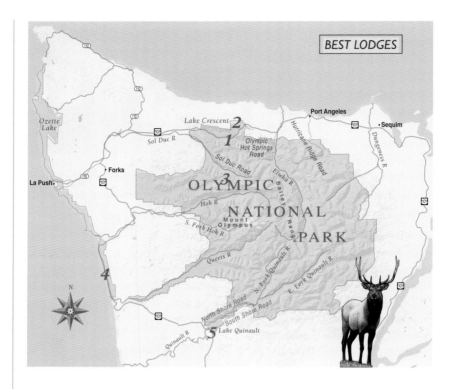

Impenetrable by vehicle, the Olympic Mountains dominate the center of the park. U.S. Highway 101 skirts the mountains, and some roads follow drainages to points of interest. Driving times from one point to another can be very long. For instance, driving from park headquarters in Port Angeles to Lake Quinault typically takes 3 hours.

Also, the park's diverse landscape, from beaches and tide pools to rain forest to snowcapped peaks, begs for time to explore. The best way to see everything is to plan overnight stays in campgrounds and lodges in strategic locations. If you want to explore the coastal environment, Kalaloch is the best option. Sol Duc is an excellent choice for soaking in the hot spring and exploring the lowland forest. Memorable lake experiences are at Lake Crescent Lodge and Log Cabin Resort. They also offer close access to the alpine and subalpine life zones on Hurricane Ridge. If you want to explore the abundance and diversity of a temperate rain forest, Lake Quinault Lodge is the best choice. The National Park Service operates campgrounds near each lodge and resort.

1. Lake Crescent Lodge

Lake Crescent Lodge offers outstanding lake views and wide vistas of the low-lying hills with Pyramid Mountain to the north. The lodge offers an ideal setting for a quiet lakeside stay, whether in the main lodge or one of

Lake Crescent Lodge, Alan Leftridge

the cabins. The lodge and several adjacent buildings are listed on the National Register of Historic Places. Popular activities at the lodge include relaxing, water sports, and hiking to Marymere Falls and along the Spruce Railroad Trail.

2. Log Cabin Resort

This site was one of the first to offer accommodations in what was to become Olympic National Park. Here, a two-story hotel of cedar logs was constructed in 1895. The hotel was a popular vacation

Log Cabin Resort, Alan Leftridge

destination on Lake Crescent until 1932 when it was destroyed by fire. Rebuilt in the early 1950s in the lowland forest zone, today's Log Cabin Resort replaced the hotel with lakeside chalets, lodge rooms, cabins, and a campground.

3. Sol Duc Hot Springs Resort

Situated 12 miles into the park, the Sol Duc Hot Springs has attracted visitors for over 100 years. The first visitor amenities included a bathhouse and dining room in

Sol Duc Hot Springs Resort, Alan Leftridge

the 1880s. Popularity of the hot springs grew, and in 1912 a 164-room hotel was built on the site. The hotel burned in 1916. Today's Sol Duc Hot Springs Resort includes a large outdoor pool, restaurant, and cabins. A campground is nearby. The popular Lover's Lane Loop Trail to Sol Duc Falls begins here.

Kalaloch Lodge, Alan Leftridge

4. Kalaloch Lodge

This lodge is your best choice to base your exploration of the park's coastal life zone. The rustic lodge is situated on a bluff above the ocean and offers excellent views and easy access to Kalaloch Beach and nearby short hiking trails. Explore pristine stretches of white sand beaches at Ruby Beach and South Beach. Accommodations include the main lodge, motel-type units, and cottages.

Lake Quinault Lodge, Alan Leftridge

5. Lake Quinault Lodge

The lodge is across Lake Quinault from Olympic National Park, near its southern border. Built in 1926, it is one of the historic sites listed in this book. The setting is quiet, leisurely, and beautiful. The world's largest Sitka spruce tree thrives on the grounds, as do many other sentinel trees. Look for the oversize rain gauge on the back deck to see just how much rain can fall here each year. You will understand that you are in the temperate rain forest! Hiking trails leave from the immediate area, and a short drive on South Shore Road will get you to Bunch Falls, within the boundary of the park.

BEST SCENIC DRIVES

BEST SCENIC DRIVES

1. Hurricane Ridge Road

Hurricane Ridge Road is the most popular scenic road in the park. You will see why as you get closer to your destination.

0.0 mile   U.S. 101 at First and Race Streets, Port Angeles
1.0 mile   Olympic National Park Visitor Center
5.7 miles Junction with Little River Road
5.9 miles Heart O' the Hills Campground
9.4 miles Scenic View Point
17.8 miles Junction with Obstruction Point Road
18.0 miles Hurricane Ridge Visitor Center

This route begins on the edge of a city, and in less than 20 miles, climbs into the montane zone, and then into the subalpine world. Watch for black-tailed deer, ravens, and soaring red-tailed hawks along the way.

The look of the forest environments will change. You will notice the differences between the forests after traveling about 10 miles. The montane is dominated by tall Douglas-fir, silver fir, western hemlock, and western redcedar trees. The understory is thick with salal, salmonberries, and ferns. As you gain elevation, the large trees give way to shorter trees that are clumped rather than growing with a

Hurricane Ridge Road, NPS photo

contiguous canopy. These trees are mountain hemlocks, silver firs, and subalpine firs. You will also see more paintbrush, avalanche lilies, and red mountain heather growing in open meadows.

The parking lot at Hurricane Ridge is huge, owing to the popularity of this grand area. Spend time in the visitor center, which features exhibits, a gift shop, a snack bar, and an information desk with personnel who will help you plan your day atop Hurricane Ridge.

Ready for a picnic? Continue through the parking area and follow the road another mile to the Hurricane Hill Picnic Area. One of the best in the park!

2. Obstruction Point Road

Drive through Olympic's subalpine zone for fantastic views of the Bailey Range and Mount Olympus.

From Port Angeles, drive 17.8 miles on Hurricane

Obstruction Point Road, Library of Congress

Ridge Road to the junction for Obstruction Point Road. This route is open in summer only and is not recommended for trailers and motor homes.

0.0 mile   Junction with Hurricane Ridge Road
0.4 mile   Cox Valley Way Trail
1.1 miles Steeple Rock
3.9 miles Waterhole
4.9 miles Eagle Point
8.0 miles Obstruction Point

Obstruction Point Road is a ridge-running, unpaved, steep, and narrow road that runs southeast atop Hurricane Ridge. With views to the southwest, it presents beautiful displays of subalpine flowers in the meadows in July and August. Watch for deer feeding in the meadows and red-tailed hawks riding thermals along the ridge. Mount Olympus looms above to the west. The panoramic views of the Bailey Range from the Obstruction Point parking lot are the best in the park. Plan for a picnic at the end of the road, then retrace your tracks back to Port Angeles.

3. East Beach Road to Sol Duc

This scenic drive begins at the Olympic National Park boundary 17.9 miles west of Port Angeles, along U.S. Highway 101. The mileages start at that point.

0.0 mile	Olympic National Park boundary
1.9 miles	Sledge Hammer Point
3.1 miles	Storm King Ranger Station
3.6 miles	Lake Crescent Lodge
7.6 miles	La Poel Point and Picnic Area
8.2 miles	Meldrim Point
8.8 miles	Eagle Point
10.6 miles	Fairholme
12.2 miles	Sol Duc River Hot Springs Road
14.7 miles	Aurora Ridge Trail (2.5 miles from U.S. 101)
19.7 miles	Salmon Cascades (7.5 miles from U.S. 101)
23.2 miles	Ancient Groves Nature Trail (11 miles from U.S. 101)
25.0 miles	Sol Duc Hot Springs Resort (12.8 miles from U.S. 101)
26.4 miles	Sol Duc River Trail (14.2 miles from U.S. 101)

U.S. Highway 101

The highway follows the south shore of Lake Crescent. High, forested mountains surround the large glacially carved lake. Sledge Hammer Point is the first pullout along the road, and the only pullout that faces west. It is a good spot for viewing sunsets. Storm King Ranger Station is located at the base of Mount Storm King. The Marymere Falls Trail and Moments in Time Trail leave from the adjacent parking area. Nearby historic Lake Crescent Lodge offers hotel rooms, cabins, dining, and fantastic scenery.

La Poel Point, Meldrim Point, and Eagle Point are pullouts with panoramic vistas of Lake Crescent and Pyramid Mountain to the north. La Poel Point also has a picnic area open in summer. At the west end of Lake Crescent, Fairholme faces east for those of us who enjoy watching the rising sun. Fairholme has a grocery store, snack bar, boat rentals, and a campground.

Turn left off U.S. Highway 101, 1.6 miles west of Fairholme on Sol Duc River Road.

Sol Duc River Road

The first short stretch of the road is through old-growth groves dominated by Douglas-fir and western hemlock. The road parallels the Sol Duc River, one of the longest rivers in Olympic National Park and the only one with summer coho salmon runs. You can see the fish struggling to go upriver from the Salmon Cascades viewing platform.

The Ancient Groves Nature Trail is a 0.4-mile loop overlooking the Sol Duc River. Stop here to walk through the firs

Sol Duc River, NPS photo, Carmen Bubar

and hemlocks that started growing at the time of U.S. independence. The verdant old-growth forest is alive with ferns, mosses, huckleberries, and Oregon grape.

Visitor services are available at Sol Duc Hot Springs Resort. It is a good place to investigate. The resort offers cabins, meals, sundries, and a hot mineral water swimming pool.

The Sol Duc River Trailhead parking lot is 1.4 miles south of the resort at the end of the 26.4-mile scenic drive. The trailhead provides access to Sol Duc Falls, a premier waterfall in Olympic. Take the easy 1.6-mile round-trip hike to the waterfall as a capstone of your scenic tour.

4. Hoh River Road

This road takes you to the most easily accessible rain forest in the park. From Forks, drive 14 miles south on U.S. Highway 101 and turn east onto Upper Hoh River Road.

0.0 mile   Junction of U.S. 101 and Upper Hoh River Road
12.8 miles   Olympic National Park Entrance
18.9 miles   Hoh Rain Forest Campground
19.0 miles   Hoh Visitor Center and the end of the road

Before reaching the park border, the road passes through logged land. From the park boundary to its end, the road runs beneath a lush, moss-blanketed rain forest canopy. Sitka spruce and western hemlock mingle with moss-covered bigleaf maple. A few stands of Douglas-fir

Hoh Rain Forest, Jenny Baker

and western redcedar give contrast to the forest.

The road parallels the Hoh River, popular with kayakers. You will find several pullouts to watch for river runners or to savor the spectacular scenery of the Hoh River Valley.

Roosevelt elk forage in the Hoh Valley in late fall and winter, spending summers in the high country. Expect to see only a few elk in summer.

After 19 miles, you arrive at the Hoh Rain Forest Visitor Center. The center features an information desk, bookstore, and exhibits. Here, you will find the Hall of Mosses Nature Trail and the Spruce Nature Trail. The trails guide you into the havens of colossal trees that are hundreds of years old, in a region that receives up to 11 feet of precipitation each year.

5. Quinault River Road

This scenic drive connects the South Shore and North Shore Roads of the Quinault River for an easy 28-mile loop through a rain forest and around beautiful Lake Quinault. The road is one lane and unpaved in some spots.

From Forks, travel 67 miles south on U.S. Highway 101 to South Shore Road.

0.0 mile South Shore Road and U.S. 101

1.5 miles Willaby Creek Forest Service campground

2.0 miles Lake Quinault Lodge

2.4 miles Falls Creek Forest Service campground

7.0 miles Colonel Bob Trail

11.9 miles Olympic National Park boundary and Bunch Falls

12.9 miles Quinault River Bridge. Cross the bridge and turn left onto the North Shore Road.

21.9 miles Quinault Rain Forest Ranger Station
24.9 miles July Creek Picnic Area
26.0 miles Big Cedar Trail
28.0 miles U.S. 101, 64 miles south of Forks

This scenic drive is through a remote area of Olympic National Park. There are several places along the way to stop and take a short hike or to

view waterfalls and wildlife. You will encounter little traffic, so you can explore at your pace. A morning or evening tour gives you the best chances of seeing Roosevelt elk.

Take the opportunity to tour the historic Lake Quinault Lodge. The

Lake Quinault, Alan Leftridge

interior is rustic, the grounds beautiful. It is a great place to relax and enjoy refreshments. Be sure to find the rain gauge on the back deck to see how much rain fell here last year. After you leave Lake Quinault Lodge, the road winds up the Quinault Valley past several small farms to a dense stand of rain forest trees. The area has giant, moss-draped bigleaf maple trees.

About 13 miles from U.S. Highway 101, a bridge spans the river to the North Shore Road. The road is unpaved but wide enough for two lanes of traffic. The road passes several farms and logged areas, then runs through forest. Stop at the Quinault Rain Forest Ranger Station and stretch your legs on the 0.5-mile Maple Glade self-guided nature trail that begins from a bridge across from the ranger station. Continue driving west along the shore of Lake Quinault. About 1 mile past the July Creek Picnic Area, watch for the Big Cedar Trail, a 0.2-mile climb to a huge cedar tree. At U.S. Highway 101, turn right to return to Forks 64 miles north.

BEST BICYCLING

Bike riding on U.S. Highway 101 has its hazards, especially around Lake Crescent where cyclists share the narrow road with logging trucks, semi-trucks, recreational vehicles, and passenger cars. Hurricane Ridge Road also can be busy with vehicular traffic, but is nonetheless popular with serious riders looking for an 18-mile uphill challenge. Except for the Spruce Railroad Trail, all trails within Olympic National Park are closed to bicycles.

Casual recreational riders have two wonderful options for experiencing Olympic National Park at a rider's pace,

Bicycling Hurricane Ridge Road, Alan Leftridge

and seeing things drivers may not notice: the Spruce Railroad Trail, and the Quinault River Road. Both routes are best suited for mountain bikes.

Spruce Railroad Trail

This walking and bicycling trail along the north shore of Lake Crescent is closed to motorized use. Start at Fairholme General Store, 28.5 miles west of Port Angeles on U.S. Highway 101. The trip begins on an abandoned railroad bed, known as Camp David Junior Road. Enjoy a leisurely 6.5-mile ride on the north side of Lake Crescent to the Spruce Railroad Trail. Venturing the length of the Railroad Trail extends your ride another 4 miles one way, for a 21-mile round-trip. The trip is a great way to stretch your legs after a long car ride.

Quinault River Road

This 33-mile loop begins at the community of Amanda Park, 66 miles south of Forks on U.S. Highway 101. Ride south on U.S. Highway 101 to the South Shore Road. Here you will encounter little traffic, so you can explore at your pace. Stop at the historic Lake Quinault Lodge and explore. Relax and enjoy a refreshment. About 11 miles from the lodge, a bridge crosses the river to the North Shore Road. The unpaved road is wide enough and passes several farms and logged areas, then runs through the woods and along the shore of Lake Quinault. Spend time at the Quinault Rain Forest Ranger Station and explore Maple Glade. The road eventually links to U.S. Highway 101. Turn left and pedal about 4 miles south to return to your vehicle.

BEST PICNIC AREAS

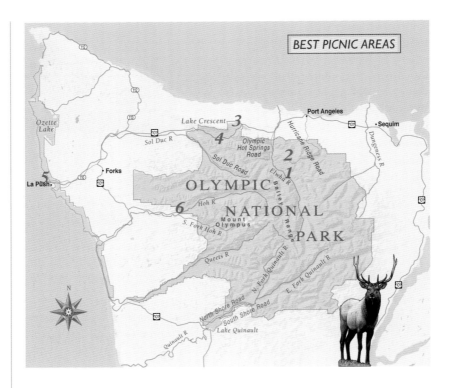

Olympic National Park has 12 developed picnic areas scattered along the roadways. The following are the best for scenery and nearby activities. All of these sites have restrooms that are wheelchair accessible.

Remember to bring a picnic basket! The Hurricane

Pack a picnic lunch, NPS photo, Rainey McKenna

Ridge Visitor Center picnic area is the only site that has food services nearby. Before you hit the road for a day of exploration, make sure you are traveling with everything you need. The next store may be an hour or more away.

1. Hurricane Ridge Visitor Center

Picnic tables are located on the lower level outside of the center. There are few tables, but each has great views of the Bailey Range and the Olympic Mountains.

Hurricane Ridge Visitor Center, Alan Leftridge

2. Hurricane Hill

Past Hurricane Ridge Visitor Center, find the Hurricane Hill Road at the west end of the parking lot. Follow it 1 mile to the large picnic area. The site is accessible and has water, toilets, and great views.

3. East Beach at Lake Crescent

From Port Angeles, drive 17 miles west on U.S.

Hurricane Hill Picnic Area, Alan Leftridge

Highway 101 and turn right onto East Beach Road. Look for the NPS sign for the picnic area after 1 mile. The picnic area is on the shore of Lake Crescent. It features a very popular swimming beach and lots of room for children to play.

4. La Poel at Lake Crescent

Located 25 miles west of Port Angeles on U.S. Highway 101, La Poel offers marvelous scenery, with views of the lake and Pyramid Mountain. The site is open during the summer months.

5. Rialto Beach

A wheelchair-accessible path leads north from the parking lot to this picnic area in a jumble of huge driftwood

Rialto Beach Picnic Area, Alan Leftridge

logs within earshot of the crashing waves. Explore the beach and the sculptural giant trees.

6. Hoh Rain Forest

From Forks, drive 14 miles south on U.S. Highway 101, turn east onto Upper Hoh River Road, and drive almost 19 miles east. The picnic area is between the Hoh Rain Forest Visitor Center parking lot and the campground. There is plenty to do here—explore the visitor center, short trails, and the Hoh River bank.

Hall of Mosses, Alan Leftridge

BEST CAMPGROUNDS

There are dozens of private and USDA Forest Service campgrounds on the Olympic Peninsula. The National Park Service maintains 12 front-country campgrounds within the park. These six best campgrounds represent the park's diverse life zones and are accessible to all visitors. Kalaloch is the only campground that accepts reservations (through www.recreation.gov); all others are first come, first served. Refer to the *Bugler* newspaper and the park website for possible closures due to weather or maintenance.

1. Staircase

Sleep in a lowland old-growth forest next to the beautiful Skokomish River. Staircase is one of only two vehicle-accessible campgrounds in the eastern part of the park, with some of the loveliest, easy trails in Olympic.

This beautiful, year-round campground has 49 sites with some up to 35 feet for RVs. Flush toilets and drinking water are available May to late September.

2. Deer Park

For some campers, the most primitive campground is the best. If that is true for you, then Deer Park is your choice. It is situated at 5,400 feet in the subalpine zone of eastern Olympic National Park. Because it is in the rain shadow of the Olympic Mountains, it receives only 20 inches of rain each year. It is in one of the prettiest areas of the park and offers spectacular sunrise and sunset views.

Tent camping, NPS photo, D. Archuleta

Access to Deer Park Campground is by a 16-mile, winding, gravel road. Depending on road conditions, the campground is open from June to mid-October. It has 14 tent sites (none for RVs), pit toilets, and is wheelchair accessible. Bring your own drinking water.

3. Elwha River

This campground is a great location for access to trail destinations like Dodger Creek Bridge and Goblin Gates. Be sure to visit Madison Falls and the Glines Canyon Dam removal site a few miles up the road.

This riverside, forested campground is open year-round. It has 40 sites with some up to 35 feet for RVs. Elwha offers pit toilets. Running water is available during summer.

4. Sol Duc

Experience the serenity of camping in an old-growth rain forest near a fast-moving river. Fabulous Sol Duc Falls is less than a mile walk on a well-traveled path. Venture further into the wilds with a day hike to Seven Lakes Basin. The Lover's Lane Trail leads you to Sol Duc Hot Springs Resort with its mineral pool, store, and restaurant.

This year-round campground has 82 sites with some accommodating RVs up to 35 feet. Find a campsite next to the river. Flush toilets and drinking water are available April to October.

5. Hoh Rain Forest

You will likely get wet, but camping here is a great adventure. The campground is in one of the wettest places on earth, surrounded by giant trees and draping mosses. Get a campsite along the Hoh River and be soothed to sleep by the music of its tumbling waters. This beautiful year-round campground has 88 sites with some up to 21 feet for RVs.

6. Kalaloch

Kalaloch is an extraordinary beach campground. Its location gives you easy access to the coast, Kalaloch Beach, Ruby Beach, Queets River Valley, and Lake Quinault. Nearby visitor services include a store, the Kalaloch Lodge restaurant, and a gas station. Select this campground for its convenience, hiking opportunities, sunsets, and beach exploration. The 170-site campground is open year-round and has some parking pads up to 35 feet for RVs. Reservations are advised during the busy summer season.

Camping at Kalaloch, NPS photo, Carmen Bubar

BEST NAMES OF NATURAL FEATURES

Here is some light-hearted fun. Review the park map for interesting place names. Look for the names of mountains, lakes, rivers, creeks, ridges, and waterfalls. The origins of some are obvious, others obscure. Many names are descriptive, while some are expressive. Most are documented, but the stories of a few are lost to antiquity. Many of the park's names are from Norse, Greek, Roman, and American Indian legends. Other places are named for people associated with the park area, or the names honor local tribes. Here is a short list of some of the best names of natural features in the park.

✐ **Dosewallips**
A campground and river are named for a Twana Indian mythical man named Dos-wail-opsh. He is said to have turned into a mountain at the river's headwaters.

✐ **Dragon Lake**
Like so many other places in Olympic, it is unclear why and for whom this feature was named. Visitors and maybe a government survey party noted the apparent numbers of dragonflies hunting along the lake's surface.

✐ **Enchanted Valley**
Forester Fred Cleator is credited with naming the place that is full of waterfalls and was traditionally used as a meeting place for Cowlitz, Quinault, and Chehalis peoples.

✐ **Flypaper Pass**
An access to the pass is by way of Anderson Glacier. Observers from afar declared that hikers looked like flies stuck on paper.

✐ **Geoduck Creek**
The name geoduck (a type of clam) is from the Nisqually Indian language. It's pronounced GOO-ee-duk. An Olympic National Forest supervisor, Rudo Fromme, named the creek after the clam as a whimsical gesture.

✐ **Goblin Gates**
This site was named by members of the *Seattle Press* Expedition of 1890. Castle gate-like rock spires on the sides of the Elwha River constrict water flow and appear to suck water through the opening. Deep shadows along the cliff walls evoke visions of animals, demons, and goblins.

Hee Hee Creek
Hee Hee is Chinook jargon for "laugh" or "happy," suggesting the nature of the creek as it merrily dances its way through the valley.

Hurricane Ridge
Wintertime storm fronts push air that is compressed by the obstructing ridge. Hurricane-force winds blast over the top, sometimes exceeding 100 miles an hour.

Mount Duckabush
The name is an English corruption of a native word for a reddish face; a description applied to local mountain bluffs.

Mount Olympus
Named after the home of the gods in Greek mythology. Captain John Meares first applied the name when he saw the mountain from his ship while passing in 1778.

Mount Storm King
Native American legend names Storm King as the great ruler of this area at Lake Crescent.

Olympic
Captain George Vancouver applied the name of the mountain range in 1792. The word Olympic has been attached to several natural and geologic features since, including Olympic National Park.

Pluto's Gulch
The ancient Greek word for hell is Pluto. The gulch was given the name in 1890 by Harry Fisher, who declared the gulch ugly and the water torrent deafening.

Queets River
Named for the Queets tribe by James Swan in 1857.

Shi Shi Beach
The Makah Indians referred to this area as *sa sayi s*, meaning surf beach or smelt beach. Say "shy shy."

Sol Duc
The words are of native origin for sparkling water.

Discover a mountain, lake, river, creek, ridge, or waterfall without a name? Give it one!

A BRIEF LOOK AT OLYMPIC'S GEOLOGY

Olympic coast, NPS photo

You can see the consequences of an ongoing geologic process as you travel Olympic National Park. Known as *orogenic uplift*, this same phenomenon made the Andes, the Himalayas, and the Alps. The process is more active here than anywhere on earth. Orogenic uplift as it applies to Olympic works like this:

For thousands of years deep in the Pacific, mud and sand that eroded from the adjacent land atop the North American plate was deposited in thick, horizontal layers upon the Juan de Fuca plate. Added to this were intermittent layers of lava that emerged from fissures or seafloor volcanoes. Over time, these layers hardened to stone.

Plate tectonics pushed the Juan de Fuca plate east into the heavier and more resistant North American plate. As the Juan de Fuca plate slid downward under the North American plate, some of its layers were scraped off and prodded skyward to form the elemental Olympic Mountains. This process began some 40 million years ago and continues today.

During a glacial cycle beginning 70,000 years ago, a massive ice sheet covered western Washington. This ice sheet split at the Olympic Mountains. One lobe of the glacier carved out the Strait of Juan de Fuca, and the other lobe carved Puget Sound. The one-half-mile-thick ice sheet recast the mountains and left rounded foothill deposits when it retreated about 14,000 years ago.

The landscape that you see today is the result of orogenic uplift, continental glaciation, and ongoing erosion. The park continues to be shaped by runoff from prodigious precipitation that erodes the high country and channels valleys, and by alpine glaciers that continue to grind against bedrock.

LIFE ZONES OF OLYMPIC NATIONAL PARK

Olympic is the only national park with six life zones, reaching from sea level to alpine tundra, each with unique characteristics and abundant flora and fauna adapted to their particular niches.

What makes the various life zones? The short answer is Olympic's mountainous terrain. From sea level, the climate cools with elevation gain. The mountains also shape precipitation patterns—the western side of the peninsula is wetter than the rain shadow on the eastern side. These differences in temperature and precipitation shape the distribution of plants and animals.

Coastal

The coastal zone is the easiest area to identify. Its western edge is the Pacific Ocean, and the inland side includes active and dormant dune environments. Here, you will find tide pools to explore, wide beaches, huge driftwood mounds to climb, and sandy trails through rolling hills. Flora includes salal, salmonberry thickets, wallflowers, and Douglas-fir stands.

Temperate Rain Forest

Inland from the coastal zone is the temperate rain forest. It is a region of stable maritime climate with ample moisture year-round, mild winters, and cool summers. The environment affords excellent conditions for abundant plants and animals and an enormous diversity of life. You will discover lush forests in the Hoh, Queets, Bogachiel, and Quinault Valleys. Moderate temperatures and copious rainfall produce huge Sitka spruce and western hemlock trees. While walking the trails, look for nurse logs sprouting young trees and extensive communities of mosses, fungi, amphibians, insects, and mammals, including Roosevelt elk and black bears. Typical flora includes bigleaf maple, alder, sword ferns, and carpets of oxalis.

Lowland Forest

About the same elevations as the temperate rain forest, but farther from the coast and situated in valleys facing north and east, you will discover the lowland forest. The microclimate is drier than the rain forest. Representative lowland forests are in the Sol Duc and Elwha Valleys, around Lake Crescent, and Staircase in the southeast corner of the park. Douglas-fir, grand fir, western redcedar, and western hemlock trees dominate the coniferous forests. Understory flora includes stream violets, trillium, sword ferns, salal, huckleberries, and oceanspray.

Montane

Upward from the valleys is the mountainous (montane) zone of Olympic. Think of it as a horizontal belt beginning at about 1,500 feet and continuing to the subalpine zone at around 4,000 feet. The montane belt includes both the wet side and dry side of the mountains. Forests on the cooler, damper ocean side often appear as rain forests, steadily dripping condensation from the misty clouds that immerse them. Cooler temperatures mean that trees here grow shorter than lowland trees, but there are more epiphytic plants because of the dampness. Silver fir and western hemlock are dominant species. The forests on the drier east side of the Olympic Mountains are mostly Douglas-fir and western hemlock. Montane forests cover vast swaths of the park's mountain slopes. Growing conditions can be tough, as microclimates are variable and sometimes extreme. You pass through the montane on your way to Hurricane Ridge and Deer Park. All hiking trails into the high country pass through the montane. Common trees include Douglas-fir, silver fir, western hemlock, and western redcedar. Understory plants include salal and huckleberries.

Subalpine

The subalpine zone is a wonderland of delights for many visitors to experience life in extreme conditions. People come here to see trees of the subalpine forests that are miniature compared to their montane and lowland brethren. It is a wonder to see how heavy snow, dry but cold winds, and a short growing season affect trees, wildflowers, and animals that make this region their home. Popular with visitors are the krummholz tree islands and flagged trees, formed by hurricane-force winter winds blasting icy snow. People also come to Hurricane Ridge to marvel at the explosive wildflower display in the short summer season. Notable tree species of the subalpine region are mountain hemlock, silver fir, subalpine fir, and alder. Wildflowers here include avalanche lilies, paintbrush, red mountain heather, shooting star, and violets. Look for marmots, mountain goats, chipmunks, and butterflies.

Alpine flowers, NPS photo, Bill Baccus

Alpine

As you venture by road or trail into the Olympic Mountains, the average temperature drops. Winter-like weather lingers so long that it remains too cold for tree seeds to germinate. You have reached the treeline and alpine zone. The treeline in the Olympics is between 5,000 and 6,000 feet, depending on the site location. Conditions in the alpine region are harsh for humans, but the fauna and flora are evolved to thrive here. You reach the alpine zone by driving to the end of Hurricane Ridge Road, Obstruction Point Road, and Deer Park Road. Many wilderness trails leading to ridges and peaks take you through the alpine region. Your explorations by road or trail will allow you to experience ground-hugging cushion plants growing in rock cracks, tiny ferns, waxy sedges, and boulders painted in colorful lichens. Plants of the alpine include spreading phlox, Flett's violet, and Olympic's own Piper's bellflower. A horned lark or a rosy finch might serenade you. Watch for the playful antics of Olympic marmots or Olympic chipmunks.

You are fortunate to be visiting Olympic because few national parks have such ecological diversity. Explore the variety and abundance of life in this truly unique region.

BEST SELF-GUIDED TRAILS

BEST SELF-GUIDED TRAILS

1. Staircase Rapids Loop Trail
Level of difficulty: Easy
Duration: 60 to 90 minutes
Distance: 2-mile loop
Elevation change: 200 feet
Best time of the year: Summer
Trailhead: From Hoodsport, drive 9 miles west on North Lake Cushman Road. The road becomes Forest Road 24. Follow it another 6.5 miles to the Staircase Ranger Station. The trail begins behind the ranger station.
Special note: The road from Hoodsport to Staircase often closes due to weather. Call (360)565-3131 for road conditions.

Be sure to get a copy of the Staircase Rapids Nature Trail brochure from the ranger station. The interpretation in the brochure will enhance your experience.

The hike: Part of this trail is wheelchair accessible. All visitors can reach Big Cedar, a 14-foot-diameter western redcedar, and the Skokomish River viewpoint. The redcedar is 0.6 mile from the trailhead, on a spur trail. The viewpoint is 0.5 mile on the Rapids Loop Trail itself.

You will be traveling among gigantic Douglas-fir trees, with a vast understory of shrubs and wildflowers. The wandering trail leads along the south bank of the Skokomish past rapids and crystalline pools. One mile into the trail, you will come to a bridge across the river. Passing to the north bank, enjoy viewing the pools and rapids from a different angle as you return to the trailhead.

2. Rain Shadow Loop

Level of difficulty: Easy
Duration: 30 minutes
Distance: 0.5-mile loop
Elevation change: 200-foot elevation gain
Best time of the year: Summer
Trailhead: From Port Angeles, drive 6 miles east on U.S. Highway 101. Turn south on Deer Park Road. Follow the paved and gravel road 19 miles to the Blue Mountain parking area. The trail begins at the southeast edge of the lot.

Special note: The gravel portion of the Deer Park Road is narrow and one lane. It is only recommended for passenger vehicles. Acquire a Rain Shadow Trail guide at the Olympic National Park Visitor Center, in case there are none available at the trailhead.

The hike: The self-guided trail ascends through a subalpine forest to the summit of 6,010-foot Blue Mountain. Only 50 inches of precipitation fall here annually, compared to more than 200 inches on Mount Olympus. The trail guide explains the ecology of this unique area, and how plants and animals are adapted to living here.

If weather permits, the views from atop Blue Mountain are stunning. You can look over the Strait of Juan de Fuca to Victoria, the capital of British Columbia. You can also spot the San Juan Islands to the north and the Cascade Range on the eastern skyline. Looking west you will gaze upon the interior of the park and the magnificent Olympic Range.

3. Living Forest Trail
Level of difficulty: Easy
Duration: 30 minutes
Distance: 0.4-mile loop
Elevation change: None
Best time of the year: Spring through autumn
Trailhead: The trail is behind the Olympic National Park Visitor Center. Pass into the visitor center and out the back exit. The trail begins at the end of the ramp.

Living Forest Trail, Alan Leftridge

Special note: The hard-packed trail is wheelchair accessible.
The hike: The trail leads you through lowland forest to a view of the Peabody Creek valley. The music of the creek will entertain you before you see it.

4. Meadow Loop Trail
Level of difficulty: Easy
Duration: 30 minutes
Distance: 0.5-mile loop
Elevation change: Mostly level
Best time of the year: Spring through autumn
Trailhead: The Meadow Loop Trail begins north of the Hurricane Ridge parking lot.
Special note: Paved its entire length, the trail is accessible to all visitors.
The hike: This is more of a stroll than a hike. It is very popular, so you will be walking with lots of other visitors. People from all over the world seek the views from the ridgeline. It's enjoyable to watch their reactions to the vistas and wildlife. Weather permitting, you will find excellent views of the Olympic Mountains and the Strait of Juan de Fuca. Expect to find black-tailed deer, marmots, and gray jays along your excursion. Several short paved trails wander into the subalpine world of Hurricane Ridge. Follow and explore.

5. *Moments in Time Nature Trail*
Level of difficulty: Easy
Duration: 30 minutes
Distance: 0.5-mile loop
Elevation change: None
Best time of the year: Anytime
Trailhead: From Port Angeles, drive 21 miles west on U.S. Highway 101 to the Lake Crescent/Storm King Ranger Station turnoff. Follow the signs to the ranger station. The trail begins at the parking area of the Storm King Ranger Station.

Special note: This is an excellent trail for the whole family. Its hard-packed surface makes it accessible. The parking area has restrooms and a picnic area with plenty of room for children to run. Pick up a trail map at the trailhead or at the Olympic National Park Visitor Center.

The hike: The trail passes through an old-growth lowland forest and skirts Lake Crescent. The forest is alive with Douglas squirrels, pileated woodpeckers, and black-tailed deer. Along the way, you will pass abandoned homesteads. For your viewing pleasure, you will find benches along the forest trail and at the lakefront.

6. *Hall of Mosses Trail*
Level of difficulty: Easy
Duration: 60 minutes
Distance: 0.8-mile loop
Elevation change: 60-foot gain
Best time of the year: Anytime
Trailhead: From Forks, drive 14 miles south on U.S. Highway 101. Turn east on

Hall of Mosses Trail, Jenny Baker

Upper Hoh River Road and follow it 19 miles to the Hoh Rain Forest Visitor Center. The trail begins at the center.

Special note: Expect wet footing. Muddy puddles abound. Be sure to bring a camera.

The hike: This trail will help you understand how life adapts to an extreme abundance of rainfall in the temperate zone. You will find the diversity of flora in the Hoh Rain Forest to be an astonishing amount.

Interpretive signs along the trail explain key characteristics of the rain forest communities. After crossing a small creek and walking up a short hill, you will enter an otherworldly environment of mammoth trees, epiphytes, nurse logs, and octopus trees. Your short stroll is through a verdant grove of western hemlock, Douglas-fir, bigleaf maple, western redcedar, and Sitka spruce. Halfway along the trail, you'll encounter a sign pointing to a bigleaf maple grove. The trail spur leads to huge maple trees draped in long streamers of mosses. The main trail loops back toward the visitor center. From there you can venture off to the Spruce Nature Trail.

7. Spruce Nature Trail

Level of difficulty: Easy

Duration: 45 to 90 minutes

Distance: 1.2-mile loop

Elevation change: Minimal

Best time of the year: Anytime

Trailhead: From Forks, drive 14 miles south on U.S.

Spruce Nature Trail, NPS photo, Rainey McKenna

Highway 101. Turn east on Upper Hoh River Road and follow it 19 miles to the Hoh Rain Forest Visitor Center. The trail begins at the center.

Special note: Unlike the deep, undisturbed soils of the nearby Hall of Mosses Nature Trail, the Spruce Nature Trail runs through the ever-changing river bottom, where deposition and erosion occurs. Many old-growth monarchs survive beside trees and understory plants that thrive in nutrient-poor soils. Expect muddy conditions.

The hike: This hike is popular, the trail well marked and easy to follow. The path makes its way into the lush groves of the Hoh River bottom. Douglas-fir, bigleaf maple, red alder, and western hemlock dominate the forest. Understory plants include grasses, wildflowers, shrubs, and ferns. At 0.5 mile, you arrive at the Hoh River with a good view of the river bottom and the mountains beyond. This is a good place to linger and watch for wildlife. Paralleling the river, you will walk across and along both old and recent braided channels of the riverbed. The trail follows the river for about 0.2 mile before climbing a river bench and winding its way back to the trailhead.

8. *Maple Glade Nature Trail*

Level of difficulty: Easy
Duration: 30 minutes
Distance: 0.5-mile loop
Elevation change: None
Best time of the year: Summer
Trailhead: From Forks, drive south 64 miles on U.S. Highway 101 and turn left onto the North Shore Road. Continue 6 miles east to the trailhead at the Quinault Rain Forest Ranger Station.
Special note: The trail is paved in its entirety, and is accessible with some assistance. Pick up a trail guide at the trailhead or when you visit the ranger station.

Maple Glade Trail, NPS photo, Rainey McKenna

The hike: The trail crosses Kestner Creek and loops through a temperate rain forest. Visitors come here to see the bigleaf maple trees covered in long, draping mosses. The forest is also home to Sitka spruce, red alder, and western hemlock. Roosevelt elk graze the understory shrubs, leaving openings where oxalis, salal, and violets grow. Look for banana slugs on the forest floor.

BEST DAY HIKES

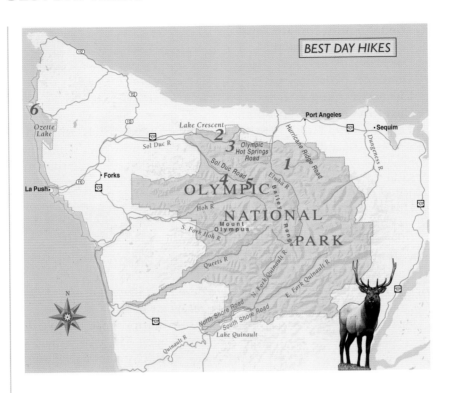

BEST DAY HIKES

I. Hurricane Hill

Level of difficulty: Moderate
Duration: 1 to 2 hours
Distance: 3.2 miles round-trip
Elevation change: 700-foot elevation gain
Best time of the year: Summer

Trailhead: From Port Angeles, drive 18 miles south on Hurricane Ridge Road to Hurricane Ridge, then through the large parking lot for another mile to the trailhead.

Notes: Hurricane Hill is one of the most popular hikes in Olympic National Park. Expect many other visitors along the path. The short and steep trail is paved in some spots and is wheelchair accessible for the first 0.5 mile. It leads to a 5,757-foot peak where you enjoy 360-degree views of the Olympic Mountains, Vancouver Island, the Cascade Range, Seattle, and Mount Rainier.

The hike: From the trailhead, the route travels to the treeline on an easy grade featuring windblown fir and pine trees. Wildflowers abound in the alpine meadows. Look for grazing black-tailed deer and slumbering marmots. At 0.5 mile, the trail begins a steep climb and breaches treeline. A switchback begins at 1.0 mile for your last push to the summit. Take the hike slowly and enjoy the burst of wildflowers in the alpine meadows leading to the summit of Hurricane Hill at 1.6 miles from the start. Retrace your steps to return to the trailhead.

2. Spruce Railroad Trail
Level of difficulty: Easy
Duration: 4 hours
Distance: 8 miles round-trip
Elevation change: Minimal
Trailhead: From Port Angeles, drive 15.5 miles west on U.S. Highway 101 to East Beach Road near the east end of Lake Crescent. Follow East Beach Road 3.5 miles to a bridge over the Lyre River. Drive another 0.7 mile to the Spruce Railroad Trail parking area.

Notes: The entire length of the trail is multipurpose for hikers, bicyclists, equestrians, and people in wheelchairs. The trail skirts the west shore of Lake Crescent for 4.0 miles, at which point you can turn around or connect with the Camp David Junior Road that extends another 4.5 miles to Fairholme.

The hike: The trail follows an abandoned railroad bed. It was constructed to bring spruce logs from the surrounding forests during the First World War. Wood from spruce trees is light but strong, ideal for aircraft frames. Rail traffic continued on the spur line until the 1950s when demand for spruce wood diminished. The National Park Service acquired the land soon afterward.

The trail skirts the west shore of Lake Crescent, gently weaving its way through mixed groves of Douglas-fir, western hemlock, and alder. The pathway then drops to the lake and follows the shoreline until it reaches a bridge across a small cove. You have reached a highlight of the trail, Devil's Punchbowl, with its deep turquoise pool and exceptional water clarity. Linger here; you have traveled about 1.25 miles.

Beyond the Punchbowl, the trail stays next to the shoreline, providing expansive views across the lake. You encounter the remains of a large railroad tunnel at 3.0 miles. The remaining mile of your trip is along the lake and through a forest to the termination of the trail and the beginning of Camp David Junior Road. It's time to retrace your steps.

3. Marymere Falls

Level of difficulty: Easy
Duration: 1.5 hours
Distance: 1.8 miles round-trip
Elevation change: 80-foot gain
Trailhead: From Port Angeles, drive 21 miles west on U.S. Highway 101 to the Lake Crescent/Storm King Ranger Station turnoff. Follow the signs to the ranger station. The Barnes Creek Trail to Marymere Falls starts here.

The hike: The trail passes along Lake Crescent, then through an underpass of U.S. Highway 101. You emerge and walk down a colonnade of mammoth Douglas-

Marymere Falls Trail, Alan Leftridge

fir and redcedar trees. You arrive at Barnes Creek after fifteen minutes of walking through this pristine lowland forest. A bridge over the creek is nearby. You'll encounter a second bridge after crossing Barnes Creek. The second bridge spans Falls Creek. Immediately afterward the trail splits, and you have two options. The left path is steeper, with large earthen steps, but it gives you the best initial view of the waterfall. The right trail is longer and takes you to a viewpoint higher up the 90-foot cascade. Take either trail—they make a loop. Walking the loop allows you to hit both of the viewing platforms. You will see two angles as Falls Creek plummets through a narrow cut before hitting the cliff face and splashing into a waiting pool.

4. Lover's Lane Loop

Level of difficulty: Easy
Duration: 2.5 hours
Distance: 5.8-mile loop
Elevation change: Minimal
Trailhead: From Port Angeles, drive 27 miles west on U.S. Highway 101 and turn left onto Sol Duc Road. Proceed 12.8 miles to Sol Duc Hot Springs Resort. Enter the resort grounds and drive west to the end

of the parking area. Turn right and follow the road to the trailhead.

Notes: This loop trail parallels the south side of the Sol Duc River to the Sol Duc waterfall. Follow the north side of the river on the return. The lower reaches of the trail are good places to look for salmon and trout traveling upstream to spawn.

The hike: The first part of the trail is through a second-growth coniferous forest interspersed with red alder trees. The area is somewhat boggy, but short boardwalks keep your feet dry over the wettest spots. Wildflowers abound here in early spring.

Cross Canyon Creek on a log bridge after about 2.5 miles. Another 0.25 mile from Canyon Creek is the bridge over Sol Duc Falls. Sol Duc is one of the premier waterfalls in the park, so take time to explore the area.

A short climb from the bridge along the trail brings you to the Canyon Creek Shelter, built in 1939 by the Civilian Conservation Corps. The trail from here passes through an open forest of Douglas-fir and western hemlock. The forest floor is speckled with wildflowers and ferns. Within 0.5 mile you arrive at a trail junction; go left. The remainder of Lover's Lane Trail passes through Sol Duc Campground to the entrance of Sol Duc Hot Springs Resort.

5. Sol Duc Falls

Level of difficulty: Easy
Duration: 60 minutes
Distance: 1.6 miles round-trip
Elevation change: Minimal
Trailhead: From Port Angeles, drive 27 miles west on U.S. Highway 101 and turn left onto Sol Duc Road. Proceed 13 miles to a large parking lot at road's end. The trailhead is at the south end of the parking area.

Notes: This hike is a short alternative to the waterfall in lieu of hiking the 5.8-mile Lover's Lane Loop Trail.

The hike: Begin your hike in the early

Sol Duc Trail, Alan Leftridge

morning to enjoy the soft, diffuse light illuminating the dense forest. An early start also allows you to avoid the crowds that often fill this trail later in the day.

The trail begins as a wide, well-beaten track winding through a forest. Notable understory plants include myriad ferns, lush mosses, ubiquitous bunchberry, and false lily-of-the-valley. Stream violets glorify the many seeps and rivulets along the trail. Expect mud.

You will hear the waterfall and the torrent through the chasm below the falls before reaching it. To your left is a path to the Canyon Creek Shelter, built by the Civilian Conservation Corps in 1939. The old-growth forest here must have looked similar then as it does today.

A few more steps along the trail and you are at the bridge over the Sol Duc River, which provides a great view of the falls. Sol Duc is one of the best waterfalls in the park. Spend some time investigating the area.

6. Ozette Loop

Level of difficulty: Moderate
Duration: 4 to 5 hours
Distance: 9-mile loop
Elevation change: 300 feet total gained and lost
Best time of the year: Mid-June through October
Trailhead: From Port Angeles, drive 43 miles west on U.S. Highway 101 and turn right onto WA 113. Follow this road 10 miles and continue northwest on WA 112. Proceed 11 miles and turn left onto the Hoko Ozette Road. Drive 22 miles to the trailhead parking lot, just beyond the Ozette Ranger Station.

Notes: The loop trail covers two very different surfaces: boardwalks and soft sand beaches.

The hike: Your adventure begins with a 3.1-mile boardwalk trail to Cape Alava. Pass through a thick forest of western cedar and Sitka spruce and into verdant coastal forests, wet with mist. Ferns line the elevated path. The landscape opens at 2.25 miles as the trail passes an early homestead site known today as Ahlstroms Prairie. Imagine attempting to make a living in this remote, soggy spot. From here, the trail descends to Cape Alava.

From Cape Alava, venture south along the Pacific Northwest Trail for 3.1 miles, investigating the wild shoreline. To the west is Ozette Island. This section of the hike features everything you can imagine about the wild coastline: tide pools, shorebirds, sea stacks, towering trees, and perching eagles. Look for seals and gray whales during migratory months.

You will come to Wedding Rocks where you can search for Makah petroglyphs. If the tide is high, use the steep but short trails that climb over the headlands.

When you reach Sand Point, turn east on a boardwalk for a 2.8-mile trek back to the trailhead. The boardwalk trail traverses expansive bogs beneath a dense canopy of majestic Sitka spruce.

TRAIL ETIQUETTE

You may find total solitude on your hike, but chances are you will meet others. Consider the following while on the trail:

- *Take time to acknowledge other hikers. Say hello and exchange information about trail conditions, wildlife, and scenery.*
- *Lessen damage to the park. Stay on the trail—cutting switchbacks and making shortcuts cause erosion.*
- *Always yield to uphill hikers. Show courtesy by stepping aside and allowing hikers traveling up to keep their pace.*
- *Apple cores, banana skins, and orange peels are refuse from human food. None are natural in wildlife diets. Refrain from leaving them behind thinking that animals will appreciate the nourishment. They are slow to decompose and are unsightly.*
- *Leave no trace that you visited.*

BEST BACKPACKING

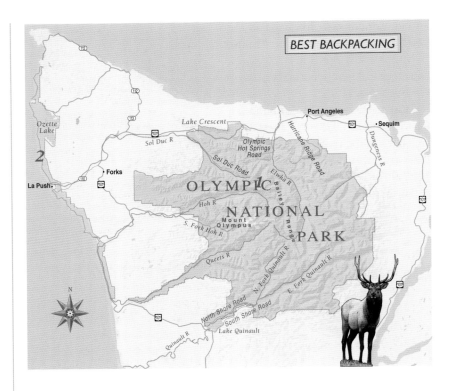

BEST BACKPACKING

1. High Divide Loop (Seven Lakes Basin)

If you have only one opportunity to sample the mountainous interior of Olympic National Park, this is the classic backpacking trip you should plan. The trail traverses 18 miles of spectacular, wild country, including old-growth forests, river canyons, waterfalls, subalpine meadows, and peaceful lakes. Enjoy great vistas of the Olympic Mountains along the way.

Level of difficulty: Moderate

Duration: 2 nights

Distance: 18.2-mile loop

Elevation change: 3,050 feet

Best time of the year: Mid-July through September

Trailhead: From Port Angeles, drive 27 miles west on U.S. Highway 101 and turn south on Sol Duc Road. Proceed 13 miles to a large parking lot. The trailhead is at the south end of the parking area.

Special notes: Mountain goats attracted to the salts found on clothing and in human waste live near the campsites. Some are aggressive. Follow the NPS regulations for maintaining a clean campsite.

Lunch Lake and Heart Lake campsites fill fast for July and August overnights. Make your arrangements early in the season to secure a site.

The hike:
0.0 mile Sol Duc Trailhead
0.8 mile Canyon Creek Shelter
3.7 miles Deer Lake
3.8 miles Junction for the High Divide Trail
7.0 miles Seven Lakes Basin
7.1 miles Trail to Lunch Lake Campground (0.7 mile)
8.0 miles Hoh Lake Trail junction
8.2 miles Spur to Bogachiel Peak
9.9 miles Heart Lake Trail junction
10.4 miles Heart Lake
10.5 miles Sol Duc River Trail
11.0 miles Sol Duc Park
14.0 miles Junction with Appleton Pass Trail
18.1 miles Canyon Creek Shelter
18.9 miles Sol Duc Trailhead

The trail is level past Sol Duc Falls and branches south on Deer Lake Trail to begin a steep climb through the montane to the subalpine zone.

Hike south from Deer Lake to the High Divide Trail. Continue on the High Divide to a marshy pond and begin a steady climb through a subalpine forest and into a large meadow. Several rivulets cross your path, and beargrass and huckleberries abound. The area is great wildlife habitat—look for black-tailed deer and bears on the slopes.

Several switchbacks bring you to the upper Bogachiel River Valley. The trail traverses a narrow path across the head of the valley and through a rocky bowl to the Seven Lakes Basin and the Lunch Lake Trail. Follow the trail down a steep decline to the Lunch Lake Campground.

The next day, return to the High Divide Trail and

High Divide Trail, Jenny Baker

head east with fantastic views of Seven Lake Basin and Bogachiel Peak. Avalanche lilies teem here in midsummer. The High Divide Trail rises steadily over precipitous slopes.

Great views of Mount Olympus and the Bailey Range come before you at the junction of the High Divide Trail and Hoh Lake Trail. A side trail leads to even better views from atop Bogachiel Peak.

The High Divide follows the ridge between the Seven Lakes Basin and Hoh River Valley. Look for bears, mountain goats along the ridges, and alpine wildflowers growing from cracks in the rocky landscape.

The trail access to Heart Lake and the backcountry campground drops sharply into sprawling Cat Basin.

Pick up the Sol Duc River Trail as it crosses the outlet of Heart Lake. The trail descends into Sol Duc Park's subalpine forests. Look for Roosevelt elk in the meadows and among the trees. The remainder of your trip to the trailhead is downhill. At times, the going is rugged, threading through tall Douglas-fir groves.

The Sol Duc River stays close at times. You will often hear the rumble. The footing is rocky, with plenty of exposed tree roots. The descent is gradually more moderate, and then you reach Sol Duc Falls, a mere 0.8 mile from the trailhead.

2. Rialto Beach to Sand Point

There are several options along the 73 miles of Olympic National Park's coastline to explore the wonders of the seaside. This 20.3-mile trail is representative of the coast and offers a wide range of features including sea stacks, tide pools, sandy shorelines, forested cliffs, pelagic birds, seals, and some cultural history.

Level of difficulty: Moderate

Duration: Overnight

Distance: 20.3 miles one way

Elevation change: 200 feet total gained and lost

Best time of the year: April through October

Trailhead: To do this hike as a one-way trip, first leave a shuttle vehicle at the trailhead in Ozette. From Forks, drive 27 miles north on U.S. Highway 101 to Sappho and turn left onto WA 113 (Burnt Mountain Road) and go 10 miles north to the junction with WA 112. Continue north on WA 112 11 miles and turn left on the Hoko Ozette Road. Drive 22 miles west to the Ozette Ranger Station and trailhead.

To start the hike, return to the junction of U.S. Highway 101 and WA 110 (La Push Road) 1 mile north of Forks. Drive 7.8 miles west on WA 110, then turn right and go another 5 miles west on Mora Road to the parking lot and trailhead at Rialto Beach.

Special notes: Don't get trapped by a rising tide—always carry tide charts and a watch! Wilderness camping permits are required for all overnight trips on the coast. Get your permit at the Wilderness Information Center in Port Angeles or the Forks Recreation and Information Center. To deter raiding raccoons, park regulations require that you store all food, garbage, and scented items in bear-resistant cannisters. Popular overnight sites along this route are Ellen Creek, Chilean Memorial, Cedar Creek, Norwegian Memorial, and Yellow Banks.

The hike: You are walking the beach where no trails exist except for marked pathways that cross over headlands. Some of these trails are steep and precarious when wet. Along the way:

0.0 mile   Rialto Beach
1.5 miles Hole-in-the-Wall Rock
3.8 miles Chilean Memorial
10.1 miles Norwegian Memorial
15.2 miles Sand Point
20.3 miles Ozette

Rialto Beach is noted for its jumbles of enormous drift logs. The beach itself is cobble strewn, which slows even strong hikers. Hole-in-the-Wall Rock is an arch passageway you will want to photograph. At the Chilean Memorial, a small plaque commemorates 18 sailors who died in a 1920 wreck. The Norwegian Memorial is a 7-foot obelisk off the beach that memorializes the 1903 wreck of the *Prince Arthur,* which also took 18 lives. The campsite here is about halfway to Sand Point, a good place to overnight if you are intent on completing the hike in just 2 days.

Between Rialto Beach and Sand Point, there are at least nine points that may be passable only during lower tides. Look for black and orange signs marking inland trails around these points. One

Rialto Beach, Alan Leftridge

headland north of Cape Johnson cannot be rounded at any time—use the established inland trail.

Wind-sculpted spruce trees line the beach. Eagles are common along the coast; look for them roosting in the tops of trees. You will also see many shorebirds. The black birds with orange bills are black oystercatchers. Watch them feeding at the edge of the water, retreating as each wave approaches. Offshore rocks offer haul-outs for harbor seals, and tide pools hold crabs, sea urchins, and anemones. Look for sea otters bobbing in the surf and gray whales from March to May and again in October.

From Sand Point, turn inland and hike 3 miles to your shuttle vehicle at Ozette.

Backpacking, Jenny Baker

BEST BEACHES

BEST BEACHES

Olympic National Park contains 73 miles of spectacular, wild shoreline with numerous pristine beaches. The sandiest beaches tend to be south from the Hoh River, while the northern beaches are rockier, covered with wave-smoothed stones. The beaches present a contrast from the alpine and rain forest zones of the rest of the park. Sunsets can be unusually beautiful at the ocean, with broad panoramic views and picturesque sea stacks framing the setting sun.

Always carry a current tide chart when exploring any beaches, and keep track of the time. Some headlands are passable only at lower tides. Others are never safe to round even at the lowest tides; hikers must use overland trails. Don't get trapped by a rising tide.

The following are five beach areas most convenient and attractive to casual travelers.

1. Shi Shi Beach

Shi Shi is the most northern beach in Olympic National Park. It is reached by driving west on WA 112 to Neah Bay on the Makah Reservation. Visitors must buy a Makah Recreation Pass in Neah Bay before arriving at the trailhead. From town, go west on Cape Flattery Road, then south on Hobuck Road, following signs for the fish hatchery and trailhead parking. From the trailhead, hike 1.7 miles to the ocean. Shi Shi is made of soft sand, decorated with seashells and driftwood. The crashing waves have shaped exceptional rock formations and created marvelous tidal pools. Bring your binoculars and look for great blue herons, peregrine falcons, bald eagles, and orcas. Shi Shi is remote, and you will sense that you are visiting one of the wildest beaches on the Pacific Coast.

Shi Shi Beach, NPS

2. Rialto Beach

West of the town of Forks and 30 minutes by car is Rialto Beach. A short path from the parking lot brings you to the shoreline. This dramatic, windswept beach is famed for its enormous driftwood, teeming tide pools,

Rialto Beach, Alan Leftridge

and sea stacks. The shore is rocky, but it's worth walking the length of the 1.5-mile beach. If you do, you will see Hole-in-the-Wall—a large sea arch—and colorful tide pools packed with starfish, anemones, and shellfish.

3. La Push Beaches (First, Second, Third)

The La Push community is home to vast stretches of pristine, scenic beaches divided by beautiful headlands. From the town of Forks, drive 1 mile north to La Push Road (WA 110) and drive west 12.7 miles to the road's end at La Push.

First Beach starts at the La Push parking area. A walk on the beach reveals giant driftwood, fantastic sea stacks, intriguing seashells, and abundant wildlife. You may see otters, seals, sea lions, and bald eagles.

From just east of the marina along La Push Road, follow the Discovery Trail, which starts at the La Push post office and connects to the Second Beach Trail. The trail is well maintained. It crosses a creek lined with giant spruce trees, climbs a hill, and then steeply descends to the beach. The broad, sandy shore stretches a mile to the south. A short distance north is a natural arch. Investigate the arch before wandering south on this beautiful stretch of Olympic National Park.

Second Beach, Jenny Baker

Offshore is a group of sea stacks set aside as the Quillayute Needles National Wildlife Refuge. The refuge is a breeding ground for untold numbers of gulls, cormorants, oystercatchers, and petrels. A pair of binoculars will bring their frenzied world closer.

Third Beach is the most remote wild sweep of coastline accessible from La Push. Find the trail about 1 mile east of the La Push marina, along La Push Road. The trailhead is well marked.

The trail is an old roadbed

Ruby Beach, Alan Leftridge

for 0.5 mile then enters a forest of Sitka spruce and western hemlock trees. You will walk almost 1.5 miles before reaching the lovely, sandy beach. Third Beach extends along Strawberry Bay for about a mile and is enclosed by two headlands, Taylor Point and Teahwhit Head.

4. Ruby Beach

Small amounts of garnet rock in the sand give the beach its name. Ruby Beach is one of the most scenic areas of the park. It is a broad shore with a rough, jagged coastline. Cedar Creek flows through the beach into the ocean here, and several large sea stacks dominate the western view.

You access Ruby Beach from its small parking lot off U.S. Highway 101, 7.5 miles north of Kalaloch Lodge.

5. *Kalaloch Beach*

Kalaloch Beach is at the southern border of the park's coastal strip. It is broad and sandy, with accumulations of driftwood and the occasional stream crossing the beach to the ocean.

Kalaloch Beach, Alan Leftridge

Just off U.S. Highway 101, Kalaloch is the easiest of the park's beaches to access. It also has the closest facilities. Drive to Kalaloch Lodge, located on a bluff above the beach. The lodge offers meals, cabins, supplies, and an excellent view of the beach at the point where Kalaloch Creek empties into the ocean.

BEST WATERFALLS

BEST WATERFALLS

If you are attracted to the sights and sounds of falling water, seek out the waterfalls readily accessed from park roads and short trails. Innumerable waterfalls abound throughout the park; many are seasonal, others year-round. Backcountry trails lead to countless waterfalls in the upper Quinault Valley and along the coastline. Four of the easiest to see during a short visit to Olympic are Sol Duc Falls, Marymere Falls, Madison Falls, and Bunch Falls. Waterfalls are favorite spots for picnics. Remember to pack refreshments!

1. Madison Falls
Level of difficulty: Easy
Duration: 20 minutes
Distance: 0.2 mile round-trip
Elevation change: Negligible
Trailhead: From Port Angeles, drive 10 miles west on U.S. Highway

101 and turn left onto Olympic Hot Springs Road, which runs along the Elwha River. Drive 2.5 miles south and park in the lot on the left side of the road.

Notes: The path is accessible—graded and paved for wheelchair use. Benches are located along the route and at the waterfall viewpoint. Be sure to obtain a *Madison Falls Trail* guide at the trailhead. It addresses the pioneer history of this interesting area.

2. Marymere Falls
Level of difficulty: Easy
Duration: 1.5 hours
Distance: 2.0 miles round-trip
Elevation change: 80-foot elevation gain
Trailhead: From Port Angeles, drive 21 miles west on U.S. Highway 101 to the Lake Crescent/Storm King Ranger Station turnoff. Follow the signs to the ranger station. The Barnes Creek Trail starts here.

Notes: Walk through a beautiful and pristine lowland forest to Marymere Falls, just 1.0 mile from the trailhead. The trail crosses Barnes Creek and then Falls Creek on bridges. The trail then splits in a loop. Take the left path for the best first view of the waterfall. You will discover Falls Creek as it plummets through a narrow cut before hitting the cliff face, then fanning out in an impressive cascade.

Madison Falls, Alan Leftridge

Marymere Falls, Alan Leftridge

Sol Duc Falls, Alan Leftridge

3. Sol Duc Falls

Level of difficulty: Easy

Duration: 1 hour

Distance: 1.5 miles round-trip

Elevation change: 15-foot elevation gain

Trailhead: From Port Angeles, drive 30 miles west on U.S. Highway 101 and turn left onto Sol Duc Road. Drive 13 miles to road's end at a large parking area. The trail begins at the southeastern end of the lot.

Notes: Sol Duc Falls is a favorite highlight for most visitors. You can feel the rumble and the spray as you cross the bridge below the falls. You will marvel at your first sighting of the Sol Duc River as it plunges 20 feet into a split in the rock beds.

4. Bunch Falls

Level of difficulty: Easy

Duration: 15 minutes

Distance: Hiking not required

Elevation change: None

Trailhead: From U.S. Highway 101 at Lake Quinault (65 miles south of Forks), drive east on South Shore Road past Lake Quinault Lodge 12 miles to the park boundary. The waterfall is on the south side of the road just beyond the boundary.

Notes: Hiking is not required to see this 60-foot waterfall. It is next to the roadway. The best views are below the roadbed and near where Bunch Creek flows under South Shore Road. You can get close and feel the cool spray on your face.

Bunch Falls, Alan Leftridge

BEST AMPHIBIANS AND REPTILES

Thirteen species of amphibians are natives of Olympic National Park, whereas just four species of reptiles live here. The numbers make sense when you think about the amount of precipitation that the park receives. High moisture favors amphibians, but the park's maritime climate is not beneficial to reptiles. These are the reptiles and amphibians you might encounter during your visit to Olympic.

Cascades Frog
Rana cascadae

These mountain frogs are prevalent at elevations from 2,000 to 7,800 feet. Their habitat includes montane to subalpine wetlands, ponds, lakes, and small streams. Winter brings on hibernation

Cascades frog, USGS photo, Robin Munshaw

within a top layer of pond mud. They become active again soon after the water is ice free. Warm, sunny days are spent basking along a shoreline or on a rock.

Best Places to See Cascade Frogs
Look for cascade frogs in still wetlands and ponds along the Obstruction Point Road, Deer Park, and Staircase.

Pacific Tree Frog
Pseudacris regilla

These are the most common frogs in Olympic National Park. The Pacific tree frog is 2 inches from nose to tip of the urostyle (the tailbone of a frog). They

Pacific tree frog, WA Department of Ecology

inhabit forested areas from sea level up to the heights of the Olympic Range. Most frogs are green or brown, but they can also be tan, red, gray, cream, brown, or black; all have pale or whitish bellies and a dark eye stripe.

Best Places to See Pacific Tree Frogs
You will likely hear the frogs before you see them. Also known as the Pacific chorus frog, their calls are loud and can be heard from far off.

Listen and look for them in most freshwater habitats in the park, from sea level to the subalpine zone.

Olympic Torrent Salamander
Rhyacotriton olympicus

Olympic's wildlands are a haven for Olympic torrent salamanders. Elsewhere they are threatened by habitat loss. No larger than 5 inches, these salamanders require cold,

Olympic torrent salamander, USFWS photo, John and Karen Hollingsworth

clear mountain streams, where they live under gravel and in the spray zones of waterfalls. Rainy seasons with fast-moving water force them to move onto land and hide under damp leaves, rocks, and logs.

Best Places to See Olympic Torrent Salamanders
Even during spring runoff, these salamanders stay within 3 feet of a stream. They are adapted to the lowland forests of Olympic. Look for cold, swift-moving water. The salamanders will be under the rock debris in the streambed.

Rough-skinned Newt
Taricha granulosa

Rough-skined newts secrete potent toxins throughout their skin, muscles, and blood. Predators are warned of the danger when newts assume a swaybacked defensive pose and emit a foul-smelling poison. Common garter snakes are adapted to the poison and are the newts' only predator.

Newts survive up to 12 years in a variety of habitats. They stalk their prey at night, feeding on salamander and frog eggs, and tiny fish.

Best Places to See Rough-skinned Newts

Rough-skinned newt, NPS photo, Jon Preston

Newts are generally terrestrial, and can be found crawling near streams and ponds in lowland and montane forests. Populations differ in their habits: some are more active in the daytime, others at night.

Northern Alligator Lizard
Elgaria coerulea principis

If you happen upon a lizard during your exploration of Olympic, it will likely be a northern alligator lizard. They live in varied habitats from the coastal zone to the subalpine

Northern alligator lizard, USFWS photo, Michael Cunanan

zone. The lizards tolerate human development, so you might find them around buildings where they capture spiders, mealworms, moths, and newborn mice.

Best Places to See Northern Alligator Lizards
Look for the lizards near fallen logs, within forest debris, among bare rocks, and in open woodlands in the rain-shadow areas on the east side of the park.

Common Garter Snake
Thamnophis sirtalis

Imagine giving live birth to 20 young at a time. The common garter snake's litter size can total 70 or more! Like other animals that are prey, they must have high birthrates

Common garter snake, Alan Leftridge

to support a constant population. Garter snakes are both prey and predator, feeding on small mammals, fish, reptiles, and amphibians.

Best Places to See Common Garter Snakes
These snakes prefer wet meadows and woodlands of the montane and lowland forest zones. In Olympic, they are most active on warm afternoons—if you're lucky, you may spot one crossing a trail.

Rubber Boa
Charina bottae

Rubber boa, NPS photo

Rubber boas tolerate temperatures at the lower end of the reptilian comfort zone. They like temperatures in the 50s. In Olympic, they inhabit several zones, from coastal to subalpine. If you startle one, it will coil, hiding its head and presenting its tail, which also looks like a head. Boas spend most of their lives under the shelter of rocks, leaves, and logs, hunting mice, shrews, and voles.

Best Places to See Rubber Boas

Rubber boas are most active at night. These are the snakes that you might see crossing a roadway or trail at dusk.

AN ANIMAL ARMS RACE
NEWT VS. SNAKE

Rough-skinned newts and common garter snakes have co-evolved into a predator-prey standoff. The newts produce a neurotoxin called tetrodotoxin (TTX) in their blood and tissues, making them poisonous to would-be predators. Yet some populations of garter snakes have evolved genes that make them resistant to TTX. In turn, the newts adapted by producing even more TTX. Because garter snake populations evolve quickly, some groups have become resistant to even these extraordinary levels of toxicity. Not to be outdone, newts increased their toxicity again, and many now contain enough TTX to kill any other predators—even enough to kill an adult human (if a person actually ate a newt).

BEST FISH

The compelling stories of Olympic's fish populations center on their adaptations to prime habitats and novel environments within the park. Two trout populations were landlocked in Lake Crescent because a slide blocked the outlet of the lake. Over thousands of generations, new subspecies emerged. The Beardslee trout and Crescent trout are native only to the unique ecosystem of the lake.

Salmon Cascades, NPS photo, Rainey McKenna

Olympic's isolation has meant that habitats that favor several species of anadromous fish have remained healthy and largely unimpaired by human development. Five varieties of salmon and steelhead trout continue to return from the ocean to the myriad freshwater streams of Olympic to continue their life cycles and to spawn.

Best Places to See Fish

Beardslee and Crescent trout are found only in Lake Crescent. Anglers may reel in one of these trout, but the fish must be released immediately. Most of Olympic's rivers support spawning runs of salmon and steelhead. The best place to see these fish is at the Salmon Cascades overlook in the Sol Duc Valley during the spawning run from late September to early October.

Beardslee Trout

Oncorhynchus mykiss irideus f. beardsleei

Ten thousand years ago, a geological incident caused a biological phenomenon that led to these trout being found nowhere else on earth. A landslide closed an outlet to Lake Crescent, isolating the fish. Over time, they developed characteristics that are different from their rainbow trout brethren.

At first, they were called bluebacks because of the deep indigo of their backs. Then, an angler named L. A. Beardslee shared his exploits catching the lovely fish. They were then named in his honor.

Best Place to See Beardslee Trout

Beardslee trout live only in Lake Crescent. The water is remarkably clear, so you may see trout in the shallows near shore. Fishing on Lake Crescent is catch-and-release only.

Lake Crescent Cutthroat Trout
Oncorhynchus clarkii crescenti

The Lake Crescent cutthroat trout is a variety of the coastal cutthroat trout. They are believed to have been isolated in Lake Crescent some 10,000 years ago when a landslide blocked the eastern outlet of the lake. Over time, inbreeding resulted in unique traits for this subspecies that lives only in this lake. Today, some hybridized Lake Crescent cutthroat trout spawn in Barnes Creek, while a genetically pure population lives in the Lyre River watershed.

Best Place to See Lake Crescent Cutthroat Trout
These trout live only in Lake Crescent. The water is remarkably clear, so you may see trout in the shallows near shore. Fishing on Lake Crescent is catch-and-release only.

Steelhead
Oncorhynchus mykiss irideus

Steelhead are fish uniquely adapted to Olympic's environments. They are an anadromous form of the coastal rainbow trout and live part of their lives in freshwater and part in saltwater. They hatch in the park's streams and move to the ocean for the next two or three years, returning to their original hatching grounds to spawn. Unlike many of the steelhead's former territories, the park's waters are pristine, allowing them to reach suitable spawning grounds and complete their life cycle.

Best Places to See Steelhead
Park waters are home to both winter and summer steelhead runs. The best time to see them is in May and June near the Hoh, Sol Duc, and Queets campgrounds.

Chinook Salmon
Oncorhynchus tshawytscha

The species name is Greek for "hooknose." Known also as king salmon, a mature fish weighs just under 50 pounds, making it the largest of the Pacific salmon. Native to the river systems of Olympic, they live 2 to 5 years in the ocean before returning to their home streams to spawn.

The Chinook salmon is interwoven into tribal cultures from California to Alaska. Many tribes still celebrate "first fish" ceremonies during the spring spawning run.

Best Places to See Chinook Salmon
Most Chinook spawn in the fall, and they run in all of the park's coastal rivers. On the Sol Duc River, the Salmon Cascades overlook is a good place to watch for Chinook.

Chum Salmon
Oncorhynchus keta

Another often-used name for chum is dog salmon. This may be because, during spawning, the males grow long teeth, resembling the canine teeth of dogs.

Olympic National Park offers excellent habitats for chum salmon. Although they spend most of their lives in the ocean, they need the cold clear streams, protected estuaries, and unpolluted coastal wetlands of the park for spawning and protection from predators.

Best Places to See Chum Salmon
In late summer and early fall, large numbers of chum salmon run in both the Queets and Quillayute Rivers. Since removal of the dams on the Elwha River, they are expected to return in increasing numbers there.

Coho Salmon
Oncorhynchus kisutch

Also known as silver salmon, coho favor low water velocity, shallow streams, and small gravel. Two-year-old males that return to freshwater in Washington are called

Coho salmon, NPS photo

"jacks." The coho salmon represents life and sustenance to several Northwest tribes.

Best Places to See Coho Salmon
Coho run in most of Olympic's rivers and streams. The two best opportunities to see them are in November and December at either the Salmon Cascades overlook on the Sol Duc River or at a small tributary to the Hoh River from the nature trail at Hoh Rain Forest Visitor Center.

Pink Salmon
Oncorhynchus gorbuscha

Also referred to as humpback salmon or "humpies," the common name is derived from its pink flesh. The color results from their krill and shrimp diet. They are the most plentiful and diminutive of the Pacific salmon. The females have evolved to stay with the eggs to protect them. Pink salmon prefer cold water, so Olympic's watercourses provide excellent habitat.

Best Place to See Pink Salmon

Though abundant elsewhere, pink salmon are the scarcest of salmon in Olympic's rivers. Over the next 20 years, their numbers will likely increase in the Elwha River thanks to the removal of two dams there. In the meantime, the best place to see pink salmon is in the Dungeness River drainage at the trailhead for the Gray Wolf River Trail near the U.S. Forest Service's Dungeness Forks Campground on Forest Road 2780 about 9 miles south of Sequim. The spawning run occurs from July to September in odd-numbered years.

Sockeye Salmon

Oncorhynchus nerka

Also called red salmon, their diet is primarily small crustaceans and fish larvae. Most sockeye salmon spawn in rivers near lakes. Young live in the lake up to two years before migrating to the sea. Some populations of sockeye, known as kokanee, are adapted to lake environments and do not migrate. In the park, kokanee are found in Lake Crescent and Ozette Lake. Oceangoing sockeyes are the third most common Pacific salmon.

Best Place to See Sockeye Salmon

In November and December, spawning sockeye run up the Quinault River. The best place to see them is where the North Shore Road crosses Big Creek, about 12 miles west from U.S. Highway 101.

THE SALMON LIFE CYCLE

Salmon eggs are laid and hatched in the cold, highly oxygenated streams of the Pacific Northwest. Known as anadromous fish, the young salmon begin an extraordinary life cycle by migrating from freshwater to the salty ocean to mature. Two to five years later, the now-adult fish migrate back to their freshwater place of hatching to spawn and then die.

The returning of the salmon to their place of birth is known as a run, as they fight currents to reach nesting sites. A great place to witness a salmon run is at Salmon Cascades on the Sol Duc River from late September into early October.

BEST PLACES TO FISH

Olympic National Park has abundant opportunities for both serious and casual anglers. Choose from several forms of fishing: surf, river, lake, or stream. Try your luck with lures and wet or dry flies. The park protects over 4,000 miles of rivers and streams,

Fly fishing the Queets River, NPS photo, Carmen Bubar

75 miles of coastline, and more than 600 lakes. These waters nurture cutthroat trout, kokanee, yellow perch, largemouth bass, yellow bullhead, char, northern pike, and five species of salmon. Anglers worldwide come to fish for salmon and the indigenous Beardslee rainbow trout and Lake Crescent cutthroat trout.

Regulations reflect the great diversity of fish and habitats the park service protects. Inquire at one of the visitor centers for current regulations, or access the information online at www.nps.gov/olym/planyourvisit/fishing.htm.

There are several fishing outfitters in the Forks and Port Angeles communities. They will help you plan your adventure. Here are some of the best places for casual anglers.

Lake Crescent

Anglers come here to catch the famous Beardslee rainbow trout and Lake Crescent cutthroat trout. Kokanee are also a popular catch. All fishing in Lake Crescent is catch-and-release. You will need to fish in deep water. Rowboats are available for rent from Lake Crescent Lodge, Log Cabin Resort, and Fairholme.

Lake Quinault

You need a permit from the Quinault tribe to fish Lake Quinault. Once you receive a permit, fish for cutthroat trout, salmon, and kokanee. Rental boats are available at Lake Quinault Lodge.

Skokomish River

The Skokomish is the only easily accessible river on the eastern side of Olympic National Park. You need not go far from the Staircase Campground to find good rainbow trout fishing.

Elwha River

With the removal of two hydroelectric dams, the Elwha River is returning to its status as one of the best steelhead and salmon rivers in the park. All five species of Pacific salmon spawn in the Elwha, as do migratory cutthroat trout. The Elwha River is a famous fly-fishing stream, especially for rainbow trout.

Sol Duc River

The upper Sol Duc is a popular angler spot for small trout, all five species of salmon, steelhead, and migratory cutthroat trout. The steelhead runs make the Sol Duc River famous.

Hoh River

The Hoh is a favorite of fly fishers. The 6-mile reach from the Hoh Rain Forest Campground to the park's boat ramp has quiet shallows and active riffles that are easy to fish. Tributary creek outlets are the best fishing. Although trout are abundant, Chinook salmon are a big attraction of the Hoh River.

Queets River

The Queets River Road parallels the south bank and provides easy fishing access. Large runs of coho and Chinook salmon and steelhead draw many anglers.

Quinault River

The lower Quinault River is renowned for good salmon runs in early winter. The upper stretches of the river are best for springtime steelhead fishing.

Coastline

Try your luck at fishing for rockfish and surfperch that roam near the park's shores. It is best to hire a guide from one of the many fishing outfitters who provide the gear and give instruction. Also, a Washington state fishing license is required for surf fishing.

BEST KAYAKING

Kayaks on Lake Crescent, Alan Leftridge

With the abundant precipitation that falls in Olympic National Park, there are many good places to kayak and canoe. Like spokes of a wagon wheel, eleven rivers radiate from the Olympic Mountains, with some of their waters held up in lakes before reaching the sea. The Hoh River is popular for Class II-III kayaking. The best put-ins are at Hoh Rain Forest Campground and near the park entrance station on Hoh River Road. Be alert for logjams and other hazards. More tranquil yet scenic bodies of water for watercraft are Ozette Lake, Lake Crescent, and Lake Quinault. Mornings are typically calm, but afternoon winds are common and can create unsafe conditions; always check the weather forecast before heading out. If you don't have a canoe or kayak, you can rent them from concessionaires adjacent to the Hoh River and at Lakes Crescent and Quinault.

BEST BIRDS

The park has six life zones, stretching from the seashore to the heights of the Olympic Mountains. They include diverse and abundant habitats for birds. The National Park Service estimates that over 250 bird species are adapted to living in the park's environs.

Birds add contrasting colors to the verdant forests and music to the sounds of the ocean and mountain winds. Olympic is a refuge for many rare and reclusive species. It is difficult to spot northern spotted owls, marbled murrelets, and harlequin ducks. Birds that are common but often overlooked are the winter wrens, varied thrushes, and mergansers. Ravens and dark-eyed juncos are abundant throughout the park any time of year. Several other species are emblematic of Olympic National Park, like sooty grouses, pileated woodpeckers, and horned larks. The following are the birds you are most likely to see or hear. The list also includes birds that are rarely seen yet add to Olympic's varied wildlife fabric.

RUFOUS HUMMINGBIRDS

Can you imagine awakening every morning weighing 10 percent less than when you went to bed? That's what a rufous hummingbird does every dawn. The bird's high metabolism means that it burns an extraordinary amount of calories while flying, hovering, feeding, and even sleeping.

Cool weather is a significant drain on a hummingbird's energy reserves, and climate change is having a profound effect on them. As migratory birds, they have historically spent their winters in Mexico. But since 1966, research shows that they have increasingly spent their winters on the U.S. Gulf Coast, staying north because temperatures have risen.

Rufous hummingbird, Alan Leftridge

Rufous Hummingbird
Selasphorus rufus

Rufous hummingbirds weigh a little more than a penny, yet they are scrappy, protecting their territory with tenacity. They establish a barrier around their dominion, feeding on its fringes at dawn and dusk, depleting the nectar that rivals might find.

Nectar makes up part of their diet, but they also eat insects. They will steal them from spiderwebs or catch them in flight.

Best Places to See Rufous Hummingbirds

You may see rufous hummingbirds in open meadows and in forests up to treeline. They can be found at the very tops of the Olympic Mountains during their migration.

Pacific Wren
Troglodytes pacificus

Apart from the rufous hummingbird, the Pacific wren is the smallest bird species you will encounter in Olympic. It lives in moist lowland, temperate rain

Pacific wren, NPS photo

forests, and in the coastal zone. Its scientific name is Greek for "cave dweller" because it often disappears into cavities while hunting or to roost. Identify it by its small size, rufous brown plumage, and incessant movement. This little bird also produces a distinctive song—loud, long, and exuberant—that is, ounce for ounce, ten times more powerful than a crowing rooster.

Best Places to See Pacific Wrens

Look for this bird flitting among the understory plants in coastal zone and lowland forests. It is also common in the Elwha Valley.

Dark-eyed Junco
Junco hyemalis

Sometimes referred to as snowbirds, dark-eyed juncos are flashy birds that flit about the montane and lowland forest floors. They are easy to recognize by their crisp markings and white-lined

Dark-eyed junco, Alan Leftridge

tail feathers they fan out in flight. Juncos are primarily insectivores in summer, then switch to eating seeds in winter.

Best Places to See Dark-eyed Juncos

You can expect to see juncos in open places and forest margins throughout the park. They can be found up to treeline, including at Hurricane Ridge and Blue Mountain.

Varied Thrush

Ixoreus naevius

Varied thrush, NPS photo, David Restivo

You may never see the beautiful varied thrush but will likely hear its rich, ringing song echoing as you stroll the quiet, mature forests in Olympic. Varied thrushes live in the wet, dense forests dominated by Sitka spruce, red alder, western hemlock, western redcedar, or Douglas-fir trees. If you are fortunate to see this demure robin-size bird, it will likely be hunting for insects in the dark understory of ferns and shrubs.

Best Places to See Varied Thrushes

These elusive birds are more likely heard than seen. They frequent the Elwha Valley and other lowland forests on the north and east sides of Olympic.

Steller's Jay

Cyanocitta stelleri

Steller's jay, Alan Leftridge

Often habituated to humans but none-theless wary, Steller's jays are a relative of the clamorous eastern blue jay. Their cries include scratchy, scolding calls and an extended variety of vocalizations that mimic sounds made by birds, squirrels, cats, dogs, chickens, and even machinery. Steller's are sociable, traveling in small groups, playfully chasing each other. Year-round residents in Olympic National Park, they cache pine seeds for winter food, some of which are forgotten and sprout into seedlings.

Best Places to See Steller's Jays

You are almost sure to see Steller's jays at Hurricane Ridge. They are often seen traveling with gray jays. Find them along forest trails and around picnic areas, campgrounds, and lodges.

Gray Jay
Perisoreus canadensis

Gray jay, Alan Leftridge

These black and gray forest residents glide silently through the conifers, and before you know it, a group will encircle your picnic table or campsite. Also known as camp robbers, they have arrived to share your food. Year-round denizens of Olympic, they begin nesting in March, when there is still snow on the ground and temperatures may be well below freezing. Females protect the eggs with thick plumage and a well-insulated nest. Gray jays are omnivores that hoard food by using their sticky saliva to glue and store food bits on tree branches.

Best Places to See Gray Jays
You will find gray jays at picnic areas, campgrounds, and lodges. They will likely investigate your presence when you walk the Hurricane Meadow Loop Trail.

Horned Lark
Eremophila alpestris

Horned lark, USFWS photo

"Lark of the mountains" is the meaning of the scientific name for this bird that inhabits the coastal to the alpine zones. They prefer open spaces with short vegetation, where they hunt in flocks for seeds and insects. To locate them, scan the barest ground around you, watching for movement or for the birds to turn their black and yellow faces toward you. Listen for their high-pitched, ringing call, given in flight.

Best Places to See Horned Larks
Look for horned larks in the alpine meadows along Hurricane Ridge and along the trail to Hurricane Hill.

American Dipper
Cinclus mexicanus

Bird droppings on boulders in fast-moving creeks indicate that North America's only aquatic songbird is present. Listen for its *zeet* call. The common name comes from the bird's bobbing motion when standing. American dippers build nests on creek bank ledges, behind waterfalls, and on boulders in rushing water. Their ability to walk and swim underwater to catch insects is fun to watch. They disappear into a creek, leaving you guessing as to where they will emerge.

Best Places to See American Dippers

American dipper, NPS photo, Russell Smith

The dipper's world is exclusive to fast-moving waterways in summer and near lakes in winter. Look for them flying low over rapids and standing on rocks at the base of waterfalls. Any of Olympic's 11 major rivers, like the Elwha, are good locales to watch for dippers.

Belted Kingfisher

Megaceryle alcyon

Belted kingfishers are fully adapted to Olympic's aquatic environments. They thrive where there are lakes, ponds, estuaries, and streams. For nesting, kingfishers tunnel into soft earthen banks over-

Belted kingfisher, USFWS photo, Rollin Bannow

looking water. They prefer perches on riverside branches where they can hunt aquatic prey by diving from the perch or hovering above the water. Their loud, rattling call alerts you to look up for a kingfisher in flight.

Best Places to See Belted Kingfishers

Kingfishers live near rivers and along the shores of lakes. Look for them at the Hoh River overlook along the Spruce Nature Trail in the Hoh Rain Forest and along the lakeshore at the Moments in Time Nature Trail.

Pileated Woodpecker

Dryocopus pileatus

Large and colorful—crow-size, with distinctive red, black, and white markings—you will probably hear a pileated woodpecker before you see one. A laughing cry or the sound of sporadic drumming on fallen logs tells you that a pileated is near. Leery of people, they spend much of their time excavating dead trees for carpenter ants, their favorite food. Their rectangular-shaped holes become nest sites and shelters for other birds and bats.

Best Places to See Pileated Woodpeckers

Pileated woodpeckers are not as common as other woodpeckers in Olympic, but be alert for their distinctive drumming and a flash of color when walking in old-growth forest, particularly where western hemlock and western redcedar grow.

Pileated woodpecker, Alan Leftridge

Sooty Grouse
Dendragapus fuliginosus

These chicken-size birds live in the lowland, montane, and subalpine forests of Olympic, where they forage on conifer needles, flowers, leaves, and insects. They have the odd custom of moving to higher territory in winter.

Best Place to See Sooty Grouse

Hens with chicks are commonly observed all summer at Hurricane Ridge.

Ruffed Grouse
Bonasa umbellus

Sooty grouse, NPS photo

Ruffed grouse are chicken-size forest-floor denizens with plumage that makes them extremely well camouflaged. They flush from danger only at the last moment, startling hikers with a flurry of flapping wings. They fly little better than a chicken and are not good at standing on tree boughs either. Their population cycles fluctuate with those of snowshoe hares'. Elevated hare numbers stimulate predator populations to expand. Predators then turn to grouse as the hare numbers decrease.

Best Places to See Ruffed Grouse

Ruffed grouse are residents of the lowland and montane forests. You will find them as you walk low-elevation trails. The Elwha Valley is a good place to watch for ruffed grouse.

Northern Spotted Owl

Strix occidentalis caurina

Northern spotted owls are denizens of the lowland zone of Olympic. They require mature conifer forests with high, open canopies and enough room for the owls to fly between the trees. Olympic's old-growth

Ruffed grouse, Alan Leftridge

forests provide these massive trees with their damaged tops and large, roomy holes for nesting sites. This same environment is habitat for the spotted owl's prey: flying squirrels, wood rats, bats, and other owls. Sadly, the recent invasion of barred owls has led to a dramatic decline in spotted owl populations.

Best Places to See Northern Spotted Owls

Your chance of seeing a northern spotted owl is slim. The birds are active at night and spend daylight hours on the nest or roosting on branches in old-growth forest. Wait quietly along a forest trail at twilight and listen for the owl's call, usually four notes: *hup hoo-hoo hooo*.

Raven

Corvus corax

Ravens' brains are among the largest of any bird species. Their rational behavior is considered greater than that of dogs. Ravens show abilities in problem-solving, copying, and engaging in games with otters

Common raven, NPS photo, Neal Herbert

and dogs. They can imitate environmental sounds and impersonate human speech. Look for ravens traveling in mated pairs and performing spectacular aerobatic displays.

Best Places to See Ravens

Ravens are common in Olympic year-round and thrive in a variety of habitats. Watch for ravens along forest trails, over open meadows and fields, and riding wind currents along alpine ridges. Hurricane Ridge is a good spot to see ravens in flight, as well as hopping around the visitor center parking lot.

Red-tailed Hawk

Buteo jamaicensis

Red-tailed hawks are the most common hawk species in Olympic, found here year-round. They vary in coloration, but most are a dark brown above and pale cream below, with brown streaks on the belly. In flight, the top of the tail is a distinctive rust or cinnamon color. Their wide-ranging diet includes voles, rabbits, snakes, frogs, other birds, and even insects.

Red-tailed hawk, NPS photo

Best Places to See Red-tailed Hawks

Drive any section of U.S. Highway 101 and you will see lone hawks soaring above open fields and sitting atop snags and telephone poles, watching for movement in the grass below.

Bald Eagle

Haliaeetus leucocephalus

"Sea eagle, white head" is the translation of the eagle's scientific name. Bald eagles specialize in catching fish, but they also eat carrion and small mammals. They can live up to 28 years in the wild and typically mate for life, often

Bald eagle, Alan Leftridge

returning to the same nest year after year. Young bald eagles lack the white head and tail. They start life as a dark, mottled brown with black beaks and eye pupils. Plumage, beak, and eye color gradually change, reaching their mature phase at about 5 years of age.

Best Places to See Bald Eagles

Bald eagles are common along the coastline. You will often see them at Kalaloch Beach, Rialto Beach, and Ruby Beach. Eagles are a common sight at La Push.

Great Blue Heron
Ardea herodias

Great blue herons seize your attention whether poised on a riverbank or cruising the coastline with slow, deep wing strokes. Adapted to both freshwater and saltwater habitats, they stand motionless or stride slowly as they hunt their prey. Herons strike swiftly with their sharp bills to seize a fish, frog, gopher, or mouse.

Great blue heron, NPS photo, Jay Elhard

Best Places to See Great Blue Herons

Look for this majestic bird at shorelines, riverbanks, marshes, damp meadows, estuaries, and ponds.

Mergansers

Hooded *Lophodytes cucullatus*
Common *Mergus merganser americanus*
Red-breasted *Mergus serrator*

Three merganser species make their homes here at least part of the year. Each looks different from the others, in beautiful ways. You will note that mergansers are awkward on land but quite adapted to aquatic environments. These sea ducks live mostly on rivers and lakes, where they dive to catch fish in their serrated bills. When they cross from one body of water to another, they take flight with their aerodynamic frames. The fastest flight ever recorded by a duck was a red-breasted merganser, clocked at 100 miles per hour.

Juvenile merganser, Alan Leftridge

Best Places to See Mergansers
Common mergansers can be seen during summer along the Elwha River. Hooded and red-breasted mergansers are more common in winter—watch for them in protected bays and estuaries.

Harlequin Duck
Histrionicus histrionicus

This duck's common name refers to the colorful clown actors in the whimsical theatrical presentations performed throughout Italy in the 16th century. Harlequin ducks prefer mountain streams and turbulent coastal waters. They

Harlequin duck, NPS photo

dive for prey that lives near the ocean bottom, and because their tight feathers trap air, they breach the surface with a comical bobbing.

Best Places to See Harlequin Ducks
Harlequins are uncommon and secretive. If lucky, you might spot one along the Elwha River during summer or on an ocean bay year-round.

Marbled Murrelet
Brachyramphus marmoratus

No one thought to look for the nesting sites of marbled murrelets in trees. People believed that these saltwater birds would likely use rocky coastal rookeries like most seabirds. The first murrelet nest was found by accident in 1974

Marbled murrelet, USFWS photo

on a high tree branch. Since then, scientists have learned that marbled murrelets prefer trees greater than 200 years old for nest sites. Murrelets feed during the day and also at night, capturing prey underwater, propelled by their wings.

Best Places to See Marbled Murrelets
Marbled murrelets generally feed within 500 yards of shore—watch for them in coves and bays. They feed year-round off Ediz Hook at Port

Angeles. Listen for their flight calls at dawn as they return to feed their young nested in old-growth stands at Heart O' the Hills Campground.

Black Oystercatcher
Haematopus bachmani

Black oystercatcher, NPS photo

A sharp *weep-weep* above the roar of the pounding breakers tells you that oystercatchers are present. They hunt in the intertidal area, inches from the water, often flying ashore to evade the surging surf. Counter to their name, oystercatchers prefer clams, mussels, snails, and limpets rather than oysters. Watch them as they pry limpets from rocks and break open clamshells.

Best Places to See Black Oystercatchers
Oystercatchers live where waves meet the sand. They are common at First Beach and Kalaloch Beach.

Brown Pelican
Pelecanus occidentalis

Brown pelican, NPS photo, Rodney Cammauf

Look for these huge birds gliding over the breakers along the coast, often in single file. Groups cruise above the surf, rising and falling in a smooth echo of the waves. Brown pelicans hunt by diving into the water, where the impact of their large bodies stuns small fish as they scoop up the prey in their throat pouches.

Best Places to See Brown Pelicans
When not actively fishing, pelicans rest at docks, jetties, and beaches. You might see them at La Push.

A SHORT CHECKLIST OF OLYMPIC'S BIRDS:

_____ American Dipper
_____ Bald Eagle
_____ Belted Kingfisher
_____ Black Oystercatcher
_____ Brown Pelican
_____ Dark-eyed Junco
_____ Gray Jay
_____ Great Blue Heron
_____ Harlequin Duck
_____ Horned Lark
_____ Marbled Murrelet
_____ Common Merganser

_____ Hooded Merganser
_____ Red-breasted Merganser
_____ Northern Spotted Owl
_____ Pacific Wren
_____ Pileated Woodpecker
_____ Raven
_____ Red-tailed Hawk
_____ Ruffed Grouse
_____ Rufous Hummingbird
_____ Sooty Grouse
_____ Steller's Jay
_____ Varied Thrush

Rufous hummingbird, NPS photo, Jacob W. Frank

BEST MAMMALS

Olympic Chipmunk
Tamias amoenus caurinus

Chipmunks are amiable squirrels. Few sights are more charming than a chipmunk sitting on a rock with forepaws folded against its chest, or holding a flower to its mouth.

Olympic chipmunk, NPS photo

The genus *Tamias* is Greek for "storer." They do not build fat the way ground squirrels do, so chipmunks hoard food in underground caches for hibernation. Their periods of dormancy can last from many days to several weeks. They often rouse during winter and feed on their larder. Hibernation ends in April with little weight loss.

Olympic chipmunks are residents of the park's subalpine zone where the forests blend into meadows. They play a crucial role in forest health as their harvesting and hoarding of seeds helps vitalize the woods.

Not by their choosing, chipmunks also play an important role as prey for many mammals and birds. If they avoid predators, they can live up to 6 years in the park.

Best Places to See Olympic Chipmunks
You will find numerous Olympic chipmunks on Hurricane Ridge and at Obstruction Point.

Northern Flying Squirrel
Glaucomys sabrinus

Twilight, and you settle before a campfire. Out of the corner of your eye, you glimpse something gliding among the trees. While you are settling in for a peaceful night's sleep, many animals are awakening.

The glider may have been a northern flying squirrel. Common in Olympic National Park, these squirrels have cape-like skin flaps stretching between the front and rear legs, enabling them

Northern flying squirrel, NPS photo, J. Schmidt

to glide from one tree to the next. They have a glide ratio of three to one, meaning that they can glide 30 feet for every 10 feet of drop. For comparison, human BASE jumpers wearing wingsuits glide at a ratio of two and a half to one.

Northern flying squirrels do not hibernate. They nestle with family members, warmed by their dense fluffy fur, in abandoned woodpecker holes on chilly days.

Best Places to See Northern Flying Squirrels

Look for northern flying squirrels at dusk in the wooded campgrounds, and at Lake Crescent Lodge, Log Cabin Resort, and Lake Quinault Lodge.

Douglas Squirrel
Tamiasciurus douglasii

The Douglas squirrel is the only tree squirrel in the park. Also known as a pine squirrel or chickaree, these tree gymnasts will entertain you with their engaging antics. You can recognize Douglas squirrels by sound before sight. Their clamorous chattering is a territorial warning for trespassers to stay away. With a home area of less than two football fields and populations of two squirrels per three acres, their territories often overlap. As with other animals, they do

Douglas squirrel, Alan Leftridge

not like competitors and will battle to protect their food supplies. Douglas squirrels and fir trees have a mutually beneficial relationship. The trees render seeds for food and shelter, while the squirrels disperse seeds to outlying areas, thereby extending the forest. Squirrels also eat harmful tree grubs and pollinate seed cones by carrying pollen on their fur. Douglas squirrels do not hibernate, and can live 10 years if they can avoid owls, martens, foxes, and bobcats.

Best Places to See Douglas Squirrels

Douglas squirrels are common throughout the lowland forest and montane zones of the park in Douglas-fir, Sitka spruce, and Pacific silver fir communities. They prefer old-growth forests or mature second-growth forests. While you are exploring the park, look for piles of discarded cones.

These are middens, places where squirrels peel cones apart to eat the seeds. You will know that Douglas squirrels are nearby.

Olympic Marmot

Marmota olympus

Olympic marmot, NPS photo

The Olympic Mountains comprise most of the territory for these delightful mammals. They inhabit the park's subalpine and alpine meadows, fields, and montane scree slopes. You will know that you are in marmot country when you hear them communicating with various whistles.

The Olympic marmot's diet consists chiefly of meadow flora like avalanche lily, glacier lily, lupine, red mountain heather, and harebells. They eat grasses too, which they also use to line their burrows. A sunny summer day finds them eating flowers and green plants until they can eat no more. Then they lie flat on a rock to savor the sun. By the end of summer, all this feasting increases fat that sustains them through hibernation, beginning in early September. They can weigh 18 pounds at that point, but will burn up to 50 percent of their body mass while hibernating for the next 8 months.

Olympic marmots are family oriented, sharing burrows, grooming each other, and touching noses when they meet. Watch for young marmots engaging in mock boxing matches and otherwise playing in high-country meadows.

ANIMAL GROUPS

Ever think about what units of animals are called? Here is a list of the proper collective nouns:

- A raft of sea lions (in water); a colony (on land)
- A herd of elk
- A herd of deer
- A sloth of bears
- A knot of toads
- A flight of hawks
- A hover of trout
- A charm of hummingbirds
- An army of frogs
- An unkindness of ravens
- A trip of mountain goats
- A dray of squirrels
- An earth of foxes
- A paddling of ducks (swimming); a team (flying)
- A murder of crows
- A pod of whales

Best Places to See Olympic Marmots

In the park, marmots live above 4,000 feet. During summer, they are commonly seen on Hurricane Ridge and at Hurricane Hill (a 3.2-mile round-trip hike from the end of Hurricane Ridge Road).

River Otter

Lontra canadensis

River otter, NPS photo

Playful is probably the best word to describe river otters. River otters are active day and night in the park. When not hunting food, they slide down riverbanks or snowfields or toss rocks into the water and chase them. Short legs and webbed feet make otters good swimmers. They can stay underwater for several minutes.

River otters routinely follow a circuit that is covered in 1 to 4 weeks. Males often travel 150 miles annually within a watershed. A family may roam up to 25 miles each year.

When the pups are old enough, their mothers take them from their den to water and teach them to swim and hunt. Their diet includes a great variety of animals that live in or near Olympic's freshwaters. Otters live on slow-moving fish, salmon, mussels, crayfish, crabs, amphibians, aquatic insects, bird eggs, fish eggs, muskrats, mice, and even young beavers.

Best Places to See River Otters

Although seldom seen, look for these playful animals in Olympic's ponds, lakes, rivers, sloughs, estuaries, bays, and in open waters along the coast.

Fisher

Martes pennanti

Fisher, NPS photo, Jeff Lewis

About the size of a domestic cat, fishers are one of the few predators that seek out and kill porcupines. Legend tells that they flip their prey and attack the underbelly. In reality, they repeatedly bite the face of the porcupine until it dies. They also eat snowshoe hares, insects, nuts, berries, and mushrooms. (Despite their name, they don't eat fish.)

Native to the Olympic Peninsula, fishers were eradicated by over-trapping and habitat loss. Beginning in 2008, 90 fishers were reintroduced to the park, and they've since dispersed throughout the peninsula.

Although skilled tree climbers, fishers prefer to spend most of their time on the ground in lowland forest habitats.

Where You Might See a Fisher

Only very lucky visitors will glimpse a fisher. Though active year-round, fishers are crepuscular (active at twilight) and secretive, adept at living undetected in Olympic's dense forests.

Bobcat

Lynx rufus

Bobcat, NPS photo, Jon Preston

Imagine a cat that is a good swimmer. Unlike your house pet, a bobcat doesn't avoid water. This partly explains why bobcats thrive in Olympic, where as much as 14 feet of precipitation falls each year.

Lynx rufus gets its common name from its short bobbed tail. A mature male can weigh up to 35 pounds and attack victims many times its weight, such as a Columbian black-tailed deer.

Bobcats fit well in Olympic, where a diversity and abundance of prey like rabbits, skunks, raccoons, moles, squirrels, birds, and reptiles exists. At night, they stalk the forest or wait motionless beside a trail, waiting to pounce on unaware prey. Daytime finds them concealed in dense cover or broken terrain, asleep and safe from bad weather.

Where You Might See a Bobcat

You might detect a flash of a bobcat in the lowland forest or montane in the late evening or early morning hours. Bobcats are loners and secretive, avoiding places where people gather.

Cougar

Puma concolor

Cougar, NPS photo

These solitary, secretive, and seldom seen animals are known as cougars in Olympic National Park. Other regional names include mountain lion, puma, catamount, painter, and panther. Cougars are every- where, though elusive. The chance of spotting one on your trip is remote. Common in the park, they blend in with their surroundings and seemingly vanish when they sense humans nearby.

If you are lucky and happen to see one, cougars are easy to recognize. They are large, majestic animals that can reach 150 pounds and 8 feet long. Their preferred habitat is wooded areas where they can sneak up on prey. These big cats are strict carnivores that prey on Colum- bian black-tailed deer, Roosevelt elk, and small mammals. Young, old, and weak prey are the most vulnerable to attack. Cougars do not make dens but travel around their home range of up to 100 square miles hunting food.

Where You Might See a Cougar

A chance sighting could occur anywhere in the park, most often in the lowland forest zone. If you do see a cougar, it will likely be from your car while the cat is crossing the road. They are easy to identify: with a tail as long as the rest of its body, the animal takes up half the width of the roadway!

A SELECT CHECKLIST OF OLYMPIC NATIONAL PARK'S MAMMALS

It may take you several trips to Olympic to see all of these animals. Start your checklist now.

_____ Black Bear		_____ Mountain Goat	
_____ Bobcat		_____ Northern Flying Squirrel	
_____ Columbian Black-tailed Deer		_____ Olympic Chipmunk	
_____ Cougar		_____ Olympic Marmot	
_____ Douglas Squirrel		_____ River Otter	
_____ Fisher		_____ Roosevelt Elk	

Black Bear
Ursus americanus

Black bear, Alan Leftridge

Their name deceives: black bears can be black, blue-black, cinnamon, brown, and blonde. They evolved in forest environments and are excellent tree climbers. Black bears are solitary animals that wander territories of anywhere from 10 to 250 square miles searching for food. Considered opportunistic eaters, their diet includes grasses, roots, nuts, berries, insects, fish, and small mammals. Black bears are extremely adaptable and can develop a preference for human foods and garbage. Bears that become habituated to human food can become aggressive.

Black bears pass long winters living off body weight that they amassed by gorging on high-energy food all summer and fall. Huckleberries are critical to their health, supplying great amounts of sugar that turns to fat. Two or three blind, helpless cubs are born in mid-winter and nurse in the den until spring. Mother and cubs will stay together for about 2 years. Black bear life expectancy in the wild is 20 years.

Best Places to See Black Bears
You can see black bears anywhere in the park. As you drive, check your rearview mirror often. I have seen many black bears running across the road behind my car. You may miss seeing them, but they have likely seen you.

Columbian Black-tailed Deer
Odocoileus hemionus columbianus

Black-tailed deer live at the margins—edges where forests and meadows meet. These margins offer the greatest variety of food for browsers and quick access to cover from predators. Deer in Olympic eat alder leaves, serviceberry bushes, salal, Douglas-fir needles, salmonberry bushes, western redcedar branches, and huckleberry bushes. When they need to hide, they bolt for the trees.

Cougars, bears, bobcats, and coyotes are the most common predators of deer in Olympic. Diseases and moving vehicles also take their toll. Fawn mortality is almost 50 percent. The life expectancy of deer in Olympic is between 5 and 10 years.

Deer are crepuscular, meaning they are most active at twilight. That's when they browse between forest and roads. Use extra caution when driving then, because as one deer crosses in front of you, another often follows.

Best Places to See Columbian Black-tailed Deer

Columbian black-tailed deer are ubiquitous in the lowland and the montane forest zone margins. A few are habituated to people and linger near campgrounds, park lodges, and trailhead parking areas.

Columbian black-tailed deer, Alan Leftridge

Roosevelt Elk

Cervus elaphus roosevelti

Roosevelt elk are the largest of the four subspecies of the North American elk. They are denizens of Olympic National Park's rain forest, and so emblematic of Washington that they were named the state mammal.

ANTLERS AND HORNS—WHAT'S THE DIFFERENCE?

A unique characteristic of the deer family is their antlers. Antlers are bony substances that grow on the heads of male deer, elk, mountain caribou, and moose each year. Lengthening daylight hours in spring induces the annual cycle of antler growth. Fuzzy skin, called velvet, covers new antlers. The velvet peels away as the antlers harden in late summer. The bone-like antlers aid males during the mating season as they spar with competitors for the attention of does. Antlers fall off in late winter, and the cycle begins again as spring approaches.

In contrast, horns are bony growths permanently affixed to the skull. They develop throughout the life of the animal but are never shed. Both male and female mountain goats and bighorn sheep possess horns.

Roosevelt elk, NPS photo, Carmen Bubar

Their common name is in honor of President Theodore Roosevelt, who set aside Mount Olympus National Monument in 1909—in part, to protect the elk. Olympic has about 5,000 Roosevelt elk, the largest herd living anywhere. In the park, they find the old-growth forests that they prefer. Their feeding habits remove compact patches of salal, salmonberries, and sword ferns in the understory, opening the way for a greater diversity of plants and animals to thrive in the forest.

Best Places to See Roosevelt Elk

Elk are seasonally migratory, spending summers in the high country and winters in the lowland and temperate rain forests. The herd in the Hoh Rain Forest, however, does not migrate—you may see them year-round while driving along Upper Hoh River Road.

MOUNTAIN GOAT

Mountain goat billy, NPS photo

Mountain goats are non-native to the park, introduced in the 1920s. The goats found Olympic's alpine meadows to their liking, and their population soon exploded to over 1,000.

The goats graze on grasses, herbs, ferns, mosses, and lichens in this delicate world, to the point of degrading the meadows. Predation on adults is uncommon —only cougars are surefooted and powerful enough to kill adults. Consequently, park staff began efforts to manage mountain goat numbers in 1981. The program continues today.

Stay at least 50 yards from mountain goats. Some have become habituated to humans and may act aggressively.

BEST MARINE MAMMALS

Sea Otter
Enhydra lutris

If a small dark object rolling in the ocean attracts your vision, it is likely a sea otter. A branch of the weasel family, otters float on their backs while feeding. They cannot leave the leftovers on their coats, so they roll to wash

Sea otter, USGS photo, Lillian Carswell

their hair. Otters spend much of their time grooming. Since they have no insulating fat layer, they must rub and squeeze their fur to introduce air to keep themselves water-repellent and warm.

Where You Might See Sea Otters

Sea otters spend much of their time in coastal kelp beds. Binoculars or a spotting scope will help you distinguish otters from bulbous kelp heads. Scan the waters from the beaches south of La Push, at Hole-in-the-Wall north of Rialto Beach, and at Sand Point.

Harbor Seal
Phoca vitulina richardsi

These are the most broadly dispersed species of seal found in coastal waters, including Olympic's. Large populations move from Canadian waters and winter on the islands off Washington. Harbor seals stay close to areas protected from

Harbor seal, NOAA photo, Dave Withrow

adverse weather and predators. However, they will venture into open water up to 10 miles offshore, which exposes them to predators like killer whales and Steller sea lions.

Where You Might See Harbor Seals

Watch for harbor seals year-round in sheltered bays, coastal coves, and bobbing in beachside surf. They often swim close to shore and haul out on offshore rocks.

Northern Fur Seal
Callorhinus ursinus

Northern fur seal, NOAA photo, Rolf Ream

Northern fur seals are adapted to live in the open sea. They feed on fish and squid, routinely diving to about 200 feet. With fur that has more than 300,000 hairs per square inch, they stay warm in the waters off Olympic. Early mariners called them "sea bears," leading to their scientific name, which means "bear-like."

Where You Might See Northern Fur Seals

Northern fur seals live in the open ocean. They sometimes haul out on offshore rocks and sea stacks, often near coastal capes and the mouths of rivers. A spotting scope will increase your chances of seeing seals at rest.

California Sea Lion
Zalophus californianus

California sea lions, NOAA photo, Tony Orr

The California sea lion is the quintessential seal, the familiar animal you see in motion pictures and circus acts, balancing a ball on its nose or leaping through hoops. Their streamlined bodies and powerful flippers propel them up to 25 miles per hour through the water. Diving, they can hold their breath for almost 10 minutes, as they chase fish and squid.

Best Places to See California Sea Lions

These sea lions are noisier than Steller sea lions. From late summer through spring, listen for barking from groups of sea lions on offshore rocks near Cape Flattery and Cape Alava.

Steller Sea Lion
Eumetopias jubatus

Though notably less vocal than California sea lions, you can still hear Stellers from afar. The females loudly bark at each other, nose-to-nose, shouting over territory. Nonetheless sociable, they crowd rookeries on preferred beaches. Females are three times smaller than the huge males. Hapless victims, the pups are often crushed when the bulls—weighing up to 1 ton—stampede ashore to secure their breeding territories.

Steller sea lions, NOAA photo, Vladimir Burkanov

Where You Might See Steller Sea Lions

These sea lions come to the Olympic coast in late summer and early fall. Use binoculars or a spotting scope to scan for them hauled out on offshore isles and rocks at Cape Flattery and Cape Alava.

Harbor Porpoise
Phocoena phocoena

A favorite among beach-side whale watchers, these porpoises are common in bays and harbors. They stay near the surface, coming up about twice a minute to breathe. When surfacing, the porpoises do not splash but gracefully roll from

Harbor porpoise, NPS photo

beak to fluke. You can also recognize them by sound. They make a puffing noise when breathing, giving them the nickname "puffing pigs."

Best Places to See Harbor Porpoises

Harbor porpoises are most common during summer. Look for these solitary swimmers near shore, especially in sheltered coves and inlets.

Pacific White-sided Dolphin
Lagenorhynchus obliquidens

Pacific white-sided dolphins are seasonal residents that travel north to spend summers in deep water off Olympic. You might glimpse a dolphin doing somersaults offshore. These dolphins are so energetic you might also see them leaping and belly flopping. The gregarious white-sided dolphins travel in groups up to 100; if you see one, keep looking for others.

Where You Might See Pacific White-sided Dolphins

These dolphins are more abundant off the coast of Washington during summer, but they

Pacific white-sided dolphins, NOAA photo, Holly Fearnbach

are deep-sea animals, rarely seen from land. A highly social species, they swim in groups of 10 to 100, often riding in the bow wave of larger boats.

Orca

Orcinus orca

Orcas are the largest member of the dolphin family. Their 4-inch-long teeth help make them mighty predators, earning them the nickname killer whales. They feed on seals, sea lions, fish, squid, seabirds, and whales. They frequent the cold, coastal waters of the park.

Both resident and transient populations occur here. Orcas hunt in pods of up to 40 individuals. Each pod may specialize in one type of prey—resident pods prefer fish, while transient pods feed on seals and other pinnipeds.

Orca, NPS photo

Where You Might See Orcas

Orcas are sometimes glimpsed from higher vantage points at Kalaloch Beach and Rialto Beach. Watch for their tall, black dorsal fins; orcas also sometimes "spyhop" with their heads held vertically out of the water.

Gray Whale

Eschrichtius robustus

Gray whales travel between the Bering Sea and southern Sea of Cortez, a round-trip of 13,700 miles. The migration is the longest of any mammal. By late March, they are found off the coast of Olympic, returning to Alaska.

101

Gray whales are immense, reaching 60 feet in length and weighing 36 tons. It takes a long time to grow that big—they can live up to 70 years. If you see them breach, you might notice that their snouts look like crusty rocks. Gray whales are bottom feeders that forage for crusta-

Gray whale, NOAA photo, Merrill Gosho

ceans by scooping up seafloor sediments and filtering them through a comb-like strainer called baleen. This action damages their skin, allowing barnacles, parasites, and other animals to attach themselves.

Minke and humpback whales also follow part of the gray whale migration path.

Best Places to See Gray Whales

From March into May, watch for the spouts of gray whales along the coast. A few whales may linger through summer, feeding at the mouths of the Hoh and Quillayute Rivers.

Ruby Beach, NPS photo, Carmen Bubar

BEST TIDE POOL ORGANISMS

Few places in Olympic reflect the range of biological abundance and diversity in as small an area as tide pools. Here in the tidal zone live myriad plants and animals awaiting your discovery. Explore with care—it is a delicate environment.

Sea Anemone

Named after the colorful anemone flower, Olympic's anemones adorn rocks in tide pools. They may look permanently attached, but most anemone varieties can "walk" around on their one foot.

Sea anemone, NOAA photo, Dr. Dwayne Meadows

Their stinging polyps ensnare food in their poison-filled tentacles. Once seized, the disabled prey is guided into the mouth by their tentacles. Anemones will occasionally invert their stomach and give it a good rinse before pulling it back inside their body. Worldwide, there are more than 1,000 sea anemone species.

Sea Cucumber

Sea cucumbers aren't plants—they're animals in the same group as sea stars and sea urchins. Like us, they have a skeleton beneath their skin. Theirs, however, is made of tiny calcified structures joined

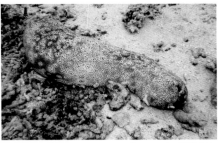

Sea cucumber, NPS photo

by connective tissue. A microscopic look at these ossicles reveals wagonwheel and ship-anchor shapes beautiful in their symmetry. When attacked by a predator, some sea cucumber species can eject sacrificial internal organs called Cuvierian tubules as a decoy. They later regenerate the jettisoned organs. In other species, small fishes and marine worms live in the sea cucumber's gill cavity. In Asia, sea cucumbers are considered a delicacy food.

Sea Urchin

These prickly animals are covered with long movable spines, yet they're a favored meal for sea otters. Otters that eat many urchins may have teeth permanently stained pink or purple by the urchin's pigments. Eggs of some urchin species are a valuable food delicacy in some Asian markets. The spines might deter you, but if you were to look closely at an urchin shell, you would see that it has the same five-part radial symmetry as its cousins, the sea stars.

Sea urchin, NOAA photo, Dr. Dwayne Meadows

Sea Star

There are 1,500 species of sea stars in the world's oceans. They invented the concept of "eating out." Many can evert their stomach, cover their prey, and digest its tissue. Then they pull their stomach back inside and search for another meal. Sea stars feel their way and also use

Spiny red sea star, NOAA photo, Ed Bowlby

eye spots at the end of each arm. When grabbed by a predator, they can drop an arm that they later regenerate. Don't be concerned for their well-being if you see them on rocks above a tide pool—some intertidal sea stars can remain out of water up to 48 hours.

Mussel

Those large, dark, glistening masses on rocks are mussel beds. Mussels aggregate by anchoring themselves with beards of strong threads known as byssus. The threads are tough and flexible to withstand wave and current action. Mussels may also use byssus threads to immobilize predatory snails.

Mussels, NOAA photo, Albert E. Theberge

Mussels filter large amounts of seawater through complex siphons. They process the water for oxygen and plankton. Their tissues absorb toxins. Scientists use mussels as biological indicators, measuring the toxins to monitor the health of marine environments.

Hermit Crab

If you pick up a seashell and put it in your pocket, beware. You may soon feel it moving. If so, you have likely pocketed a hermit crab.

These close cousins of true crabs need larger shells as they grow, discarding their cramped quarters for new ones. A twist in their abdomen

Hermit crab, NOAA photo, Jan Haaga

allows them to fit even the spiral twist of a snail shell. Trading homes gives rise to its name of "hermit" crab.

They have been known to live 20 years under ideal conditions. Their best chances of doing so are in undisturbed tide pools.

BEST FERNS

There are 17 distinct species and numerous subspecies and varieties of ferns common to Olympic National Park. At first glance, they all look the same—green. Here are four ferns that you can identify by closer observance:

Fern fronds, Alan Leftridge

- If it is growing on maple trees, it's a licorice fern.
- If it is delicate and growing near running water, it's a maidenhair fern.
- If it has fronds up to 3 feet, it's a sword fern.
- If it has ladder-like fronds that grow straight up, it's a deer fern.

The autumn season enlivens the forest floors and roadsides as it paints many of the ferns yellow and then bronze. Make sure that you note the ferns when you visit during this special time of year.

Deer Fern
Blechnum spicant

The Greek word *Blechnum* means "hardy fern," while *spicant* means "like a spike." This fern grows best in moist places with dense shade, from the coastal zone to the montane. Deer browse on these ferns, and after the deer's antlers drop, they rub the sore stubs on the fronds.

Deer fern, Alan Leftridge

Best Places to See Deer Ferns
Deer ferns are found throughout much of the park—look for them along woodland trails in river valleys and similarly moist environments.

Sword Fern
Polystichum munitum

Sword ferns are known as "kings of Northwest ferns" because of their impressive stature and sheer abundance. Adapted to almost any site condition in the rain forest and montane zones, they especially love acidic soils and grow well around conifers. As older fronds die, they provide prime amphibian cover around their base.

Sword fern, Alan Leftridge

Best Places to See Sword Ferns
Sword ferns are common throughout Olympic's rain forests from lowlands to the montane zone, particularly where western hemlock and western redcedar grow. Enjoy walking through the tall sprays of sword ferns along the Hoh River Trail.

Maidenhair Fern
Adiantum aleuticum

"Not wetting" is the meaning of the Greek word *Adiantum*. It refers to this fern's ability to shed water from its fronds. The fern is adapted to this because it lives in rocky areas near stream banks and cliffs in the spray zone of waterfalls.

Maidenhair fern, NPS photo

Best Places to See Maidenhair Ferns
Look for this delicate, eye-catching fern wherever you encounter fast-running water (especially waterfalls and cascades) in the montane and rain forest zones.

Licorice fern, Alan Leftridge

Licorice fern
Polypodium glycyrrhiza

Licorice ferns have a reputation as a prized wild delicacy. The rhizomes hold a potent compound, which is estimated to be 3,000 times sweeter than sucrose. They are epiphytes—they grow attached to other plants rather than directly in soil, taking nutrients from the air and rain.

Best Places to See Licorice Ferns

Look for licorice ferns growing on bigleaf maples, logs, rock slabs, and moss-covered soil in temperate rain forests in the Hoh, Queets, and Quinault Valleys.

LICHENS

Fringed moon lichen, NPS photo, D. Archuleta

You will find lichens living in the alpine zone, the valley floors, and every environment in between. Black-tailed deer rely on some varieties for sustenance, and northern flying squirrels get water by eating lichens hanging from trees. Varieties living on rocks display many colors, textures, and growth designs that may have been developing for a century. Look for nature's rock art as you walk the trails.

BEST WILDFLOWERS

Avalanche Lily
Erythronium montanum

Common in Olympic National Park, this lily is often associated with its cousin the glacier lily (*Erythronium grandiflorum*). You will find this subalpine perennial blooming mid-spring well into summer in damp meadows at mid to high elevations. Its erect stem topped with a glistening white flower presents an outstanding display of floral beauty.

Avalanche lily, Alan Leftridge

Where You Can Find Avalanche Lilies

Soon after snowmelt, look for patches of avalanche lilies in both forested and open areas along the upper reaches of Hurricane Ridge Road.

Beargrass
Xerophyllum tenax

Northwest legend is that when bears emerge from hibernation they seek high, sunny ridges looking for beargrass that they eat with gusto, hence its common name.

The rootstock might be edible, but not the leaves. The generic name is Greek for "dry leaf," and its specific name means "tough." Only the flower stalks are edible. If you see beargrass' tall stalks with missing flower heads, know that squirrels and chipmunks have cut down the fresh, fragrant flower stalks to eat them.

Beargrass, Linda Duvanich

Individual plants bloom every 3 to 15 years; if you are lucky, you will see a whole field of beargrass blooming. It's a beautiful, photogenic sight!

Where You Can Find Beargrass Flowers

Late springtime displays of beargrass often occur near Lake Quinault and Cushman. In August, you might find patches of beargrass blooming in abundance at Deer Lake and the Seven Lakes Basin.

Bunchberry, Alan Leftridge

Bunchberry
Cornus Canadensis

One of the most attractive native wild-flowers in the park, this woodland plant often forms an expansive blanket within the dappled shade of a canopy of trees. Its relatives in the dogwood family are, for the most part, trees and shrubs, leaving bunchberry to be sometimes referred to as creeping dogwood because of its carpet-like mat.

Vivid scarlet berries replace the flowers in late summer. Later, the leaves develop red-tinted veins that pepper the forest floor in large, vibrant swaths.

Where You Can Find Bunchberry
Look for bunchberry blooming and with fruit near Sol Duc Hot Springs and along the trails at Rialto, Ruby, and Shi Shi Beaches.

Oxalis, Alan Leftridge

Oxalis
Oxalis spp.

That patch of low plants—Irish shamrock look-alikes—you just discovered is a cluster of oxalis, also known as wood sorrel. There are 875 species of oxalis, but the one you found is likely Oregon oxalis. Native to Washington, it blankets cool, moist Douglas-fir and coastal forest floors. So well adapted are the plants to shady environments that their leaves are evolved to fold downward when struck by direct sunlight, protecting them from damage.

Where You Can Find Oxalis
You will find mats of oxalis along trails in the Hoh, Queets, and Quinault Valleys.

Trillium

Trillium ovatum

Wake robin is another common name for trillium. Since the mid-1500s, people have used this nickname because trillium flowers in early spring around the time of the robins' migratory arrival. Other names include woodlily and trinity flower. Widespread in Olympic's damp forests, it is one of the park's most elegant understory plants.

Trillium, NPS photo

Where You Can Find Trillium

Look for the distinctive white flowers in cool, moist, mixed-coniferous forests. It often grows under the boughs of Douglas-fir trees, but also thrives in the shade of western redcedar, western hemlock, and Sitka spruce.

Glacier Lily

Erythronium grandiflorum

Capable of generating heat through stored carbohydrates, glacier lilies can melt snow, pushing through the last inch or two to bloom. Other plants emerge along the edges of melting snowfields and within 10 weeks complete their annual growth cycle.

Called snow lilies in some places, their bulbs are tasty to rodents and bears, while deer, elk, and mountain goats consume their seedpods. Some people who have eaten the bulbs say they taste like green beans.

Glacier lily, Alan Leftridge

These delicate plants can withstand Olympic's fierce subalpine winters, but not the weight of a child's step. The slightest pressure will kill the bulb.

Where You Can Find Glacier Lilies

Look for this abundant perennial along Hurricane Ridge Road in meadows and open forest settings as the snow melts.

Sand-dwelling Wallflower
Erysimum arenicola

The sand-dwelling wallflower is one of the most fragrant and colorful wildflowers to adorn the Olympic high country. A member of the mustard family, it is also known as the Cascade wallflower or the mountain wallflower. It is adapted to many environments, including open, gravelly ridges, talus slopes, and rock crevasses in the montane, subalpine, and alpine life zones.

Sand-dwelling wallflower, Alan Leftridge

Where You Can Find Sand-dwelling Wallflowers

You can spot patches of sand-dwelling wallflowers in Deer Park, on Mount Angeles, and along Hurricane Ridge Road.

Stonecrop
Sedum divergens

Stonecrop plants adorned with showy yellow flowers speckle the gravelly, nutrient-poor soil in the high country. Their pulpy, water-storing leaves enable them to flourish in windy, cold, searingly sunlit, droughty conditions. The genus name, *Sedum*, is from the Latin term *sedere*, "to sit," referring to their low-spreading trait.

Where You Can Find Stonecrop

You will see stonecrop thriving in exposed rocky soil along Hurricane Ridge Road and the road to Obstruction Point.

Stonecrop, Alan Leftridge

Monkeyflower
Mimulus lewisii
Mimulus tilingii

Lewis monkeyflower (pink) and mountain monkeyflower (yellow) are abundant in Olympic. Their common name refers to the flowers resembling small monkey-like faces. *Mimulus* alludes to an actor in a farce or mime, and *lewisii* honors Meriwether Lewis

Monkeyflower, NPS photo, Keir Morse

of the Corps of Discovery. Botanist Heinrich Tiling (1818–1871) drew the honor of discovering the yellow monkeyflower, and it carries the species name after him, *tilingii*.

Where You Can Find Monkeyflowers
Both species favor streamside habitats and moist areas at all elevations. Look for yellow or pink monkeyflowers wherever your path crosses a stream.

Tiger Lily
Lilium columbianum

Even traveling U.S. Highway 101 at highway speeds, you will notice this spectacular perennial growing along the roadway and in open meadows. Native to the Pacific Northwest, it is locally common, blooming from July to August. This is the same lily that you may have in your perennial garden, also known as the Columbian lily.

Where You Can Find Tiger Lilies
The tiger lily grows in moist soils in meadows, thickets, and conifer forests up to 6,000 feet above sea level. Look for an

Tiger lily, NPS photo

abundant flowering display midsummer near the end of Hurricane Ridge Road.

Harebell
Campanula rotundifolia

European folklore related that harebell plants grew in places that hares lived, or that witches used its flower juices to change themselves into hares. These stories accounted for its common name.

This delicate-appearing flower is resilient and found throughout Olympic, even on mountainsides up to 7,000 feet. It is adapted to a variety of habitats and can be found in full sun or shade, dry or moist soils, and in forests, meadows, cliffs, lake beaches, and sand dune areas, as well as roadside gravels.

Harebell, Alan Leftridge

Where You Can Find Harebells

Look for single plants and clusters of harebells growing along U.S. Highway 101, Hurricane Ridge Road, and Obstruction Point.

Lupine
Lupinus sericeus

Botanists faulted this perennial with devouring soil nutrients and gave it the name *Lupinus*, Latin for "wolf." Further research, however, showed that lupine plants preferred poor soil, rather than made it. The plant works with mycorrhizal fungi to create the soil nutrients it needs.

Lupine flowers are very common in Olympic. The flowers are blue, but white spots on their upper petals indicate that their nectar is new. Bumblebees feed on the freshest flowers, thereby transferring only the best pollen. As the flowers age, the spots turn

Lupine, Alan Leftridge

magenta, telling the bees that the nectar is past its prime.

Where You Can Find Lupine

You will see large areas of showy lupine blooming in dense clumps throughout the springtime and summer along Hurricane Ridge Road,

Obstruction Point, and U.S. Highway 101, where they grow in the dry, rocky roadside soils.

Spreading Phlox
Phlox diffusa

Spreading phlox, NPS photo

Observe the flowers and note that the center area is not the same color as the five petals. This forms a bulls-eye, announcing to butterflies and moths that here is where you will find the nectar. The flower is adapted to dust pollen on the insects as they feast.

Spreading phlox plants grow in thick mats on dry, rocky soil. The plants bloom until late August in the alpine areas of Olympic. The flowers appear as white, pink, or faded violet.

Where You Can Find Spreading Phlox
Spreading phlox are found on high alpine ridges and in dry, rocky soils along Hurricane Ridge, in the Seven Lakes Basin, and at Deer Park.

Silky Phacelia
Phacelia sericea

Widespread in Olympic, silky phacelia is one of the most photogenic and easily recognized wildflowers in the park. The common name comes from the silvery, fine, short hairs that cover the stems and leaves.

Where You Can Find Silky Phacelia
Look for silky phacelia in July and August along the roadway to Obstruction Point, and on open, dry hillsides at elevations from 3,000 to 8,000 feet.

Silky phacelia, Alan Leftridge

Stream Violet
Viola glabella

Look for the dark purple lines on the lower three petals of the flower. These lines guide pollinators like honeybees, some butterflies, and other

Stream violet, Alan Leftridge

insects to their prize. After pollination, the seeds of stream violets develop in capsules that dry and curl. When sufficiently dry, the capsules burst open, flinging the seeds all around. That is why you will find stream violets growing in clusters.

Where You Can Find Stream Violets

Look for stream violets in damp roadside ditches, stream borders, seepage areas, and in moist subalpine meadows.

Shooting Star
Dodecatheon pulchellum

Look closely at a shooting star flower. See that there's no landing platform for insects. Shooting stars are "buzz pollinators." They release pollen from their stamens only from violent shaking. A visiting bumblebee must cling to the flower, thus releasing the pollen with its vibrating wings.

Shooting star, NPS photo, Jacob W. Frank

Where You Can Find Shooting Stars

Expect to find shooting stars in wet areas of the subalpine zone in early June, and through July at alpine elevations. Hurricane Ridge Road and the road to Obstruction Point are good places.

Calypso Orchid
Calypso bulbosa

This orchid is also known as fairy slipper, or lady's slipper. These names refer to its delicate beauty. Calypso was a nymph in

Calypso orchid, NPS photo, Jacob W. Frank

Homer's *Odyssey* who enchanted Odysseus to stay with her on her island to make him her immortal husband. Calypso orchids live no more than 5 years and are susceptible to disturbances. Step near them with care.

Where You Can Find Calypso Orchids
Look for calypso orchids blooming during May and June in cool, deep-shaded forest areas.

Paintbrush
Castilleja spp.

This showy perennial is named for its colorful, ragged bracts that appear to have been dipped in paint, including red, orange, yellow, and white. Paintbrush's true flowers are tiny, long, narrow tubes hidden within the bracts. Hummingbirds drink its nectar from the tubes. Many botanists believe that paintbrush plants and hummingbirds co-evolved. Don't look for paintbrush in your local nursery. It does not domesticate and tends to parasitize the roots of other plants to obtain nutrients.

Paintbrush, Alan Leftridge

Where You Can Find Paintbrush
Paintbrush plants flower in profusion near treeline in August and September, but can be found at any elevation down to sea level, usually singly or in small clusters.

BUNCHBERRY

This small, unassuming plant spreads pollen in a way that defies imagination. The flowers have elastic petals that flip backward, releasing wiry filaments that snap upward and fling the pollen. The motion is so quick that a camera able to shoot 10,000 frames per second is needed to capture the event. The microspores discharge from the flower at a velocity 800 times greater than the acceleration of a launching space rocket.

BEST SHRUBS

Olympic National Park abounds in beautiful wildflower displays. The wildflowers are mostly perennials, but some are annuals or biennials, and all are soft-stemmed. The bushy flowering plants that you encounter that have woody stems are shrubs. The characteristic showy shrubs you will see in different life zones are huckleberries, oceanspray, red mountain heather, salal, and salmonberry.

Huckleberry

> *Vaccinium membranaceum*
> *(mountain huckleberry)*
> *Vaccinium deliciosum*
> *(Cascade huckleberry)*
> *Vaccinium parvifolium*
> *(red huckleberry)*

Huckleberry, NPS photo, Deby Dixon

Survival for a black bear means access to any of the three huckleberry species that grow in the park. The berries provide up to one-third of a bear's nourishment during late summer as the bears gorge themselves on the sweet and tart fruit. They rely on the high sugar content in the berries to help them put on fat for winter slumber. If pregnant bears do not get enough sugar from the huckleberries, they will give birth to fewer cubs.

Where You Can Find Huckleberries

The fruit ripens during July in the lowland and montane life zones, and from August to mid-September in the subalpine reaches of the Olympics.

Oceanspray

> *Holodiscus discolor*

Oceanspray is an attention-grabbing shrub with hanging, creamy white plumes up to 10 inches long. It is deciduous, thriving in a variety of habitats in the park, including the wet coastal forests, dry open sites, and cool mountainsides. Oceanspray seems to prefer Douglas-fir-dominated forests, where it

Oceanspray, NPS, David Astudillo

grows up to 15 feet tall. The flower plumes have a pleasant scent detectable from 30 feet on a windless day.

Where You Can Find Oceanspray

Discover the fragrance and beauty of oceanspray flowers from May to July around Lake Crescent and the Elwha entrance to the park.

Red mountain heather, Alan Leftridge

Red Mountain Heather
Phyllodoce empetriformis

Carl Linnaeus, who devised the foundation of today's biological naming system, started the practice of naming members of the heath (heather) family after Greek mythological nymphs and goddesses. Nymphs were known as beautiful young maidens. The genus *Phyllodoce* is named for a sea nymph.

You will not find mountain heather growing in water, however. Instead, this low-growing mat is common in Olympic's alpine zone. Look for its rich, evergreen needle–like leaves with attractive purplish flowers growing among rock outcroppings.

Where You Can Find Red Mountain Heather

Look for mountain heather in early summer along the upper reaches of Hurricane Ridge Road.

Salal
Gaultheria shallon

If you have ever received a flower arrangement, you will recognize this plant. Its leaves remain deep green and shiny all year, making it a favorite of florists. Salal is also a backdrop in Northwest woods, and so

Salal, Alan Leftridge

pervasive that most people ignore it. The floral industry pays close attention though, as salal is harvested and shipped worldwide from the Pacific Northwest. Meriwether Lewis also noted it. He was the first

Euro-American to collect salal, taking a sample at Fort Clatsop, Oregon, in January 1806.

Where You Can Find Salal

Salal grows in thickets near the coast in Douglas-fir forests. Observe its unique, showy, urn-like blossoms in spring and early summer. You will find it along the trail to Rialto Beach, above Ruby Beach, and at the Kalaloch Beach overlook.

Salmonberry

Rubus spectabilis

This shrub is a common sight if you are exploring forested wetlands, stream margins, or disturbed areas. Salmonberries are especially fond of Olympic's coastal forests. You will find the raspberry-like fruits tempting

Salmonberry, NPS photo, Deby Dixon

but bland tasting. Best to leave the nourishment of the berries to the myriad birds and mammals, who are less concerned about the lack of flavor.

Where You Can Find Salmonberries

Salmonberry shrubs are common along streamsides under stands of red alder where they form large, impenetrable thickets up to 12 feet high. Look for them at Olympic Hot Springs, Barnes Creek, and along the Pacific Coast.

BEST TREES

Excellent tree-growing conditions abound in Olympic National Park. Whether you are exploring the coast, rain forests, drier eastern slopes, or the subalpine zone, you will find extraordinary samples of several tree varieties native to the Northwest. The growing situations are so ideal in many locales that some of the trees are the largest of their kind in the entire United States.

Olympic is home to five types of forest, each blending gradually into the next: coastal, temperate rain forest, lowland, montane, and subalpine.

The lowest elevation forest is, of course, the coastal. Here, Sitka spruce, western hemlock, and western redcedar dominate the wet environment.

Inward from the coastal zone is the temperate rain forest. Its west-facing valleys gather lots of rain. Similar to the coast, temperatures are moderate and summertime fog is common until late afternoon. Sitka spruce and western hemlock remain the dominant trees, but Douglas-fir and western redcedar are also common.

Farther inland and at higher elevations above the fog-shrouded, rain forest valleys are the lowland forests. Sitka spruce trees give way to grand firs, western hemlock, and some stands of Douglas-fir. Drier conditions, especially on the eastern side of the park, allow intermittent fires to rejuvenate the forest.

If silver fir trees are present, you have moved into the montane zone. The transition from the lowland forest is gradual, and in the drier eastern parts of Olympic, the montane appears much like the lowland forest.

Higher elevations take you to cooler temperatures and precipitation that may fall as snow. The growing season is shorter and so are the trees. Subalpine fir, mountain hemlock, and Alaska cedar groves mark the subalpine zone. The lower sections of this region consist of continuous forests, while the upper reaches are dotted with krummholz tree islands and misshapen dwarf trees that may be 100 years old. Spectacular wildflower displays in open meadows, such as at Hurricane Ridge, will delight you during the short growing season. Above treeline is the alpine zone. The dry, windy, cold climate here does not support tree growth, and the forests end.

The five forest zones in Olympic National Park provide a level of diversity that few national parks share. The abundance of life forms is staggering, and botanists continue to find new varieties of plants and animals dependent upon the forest trees. Explore every forest zone and experience the wonder that the trees offer.

Alder

Sitka Alnus viridis
Red Alnus rubra

Red alder, NPS photo

Alder trees are a vital link in forest succession. They thrive where soils are disturbed by avalanches, stream bank erosion, and flood deposition. Their root nodes fix nitrogen from the atmosphere to the soil, thus providing nutrients for subsequent plant life. They are common on exposed rocky sites following the retreat of mountain glaciers. Alder trees pave the way for the next generation of trees that need nitrogen to survive.

Where You Can Find Alder

Both Sitka and red alder trees are associates of Douglas-fir, western hemlock, western redcedar, Sitka spruce, and bigleaf maple trees. Look for alder trees in disturbed areas in the lowland forest zone.

Bigleaf Maple

Acer macrophyllum

The bigleaf is the only large maple native to the West. Its jumbo leaves make it the most recognizable tree in the park. Overlay your hand on one of its leaves and see how many it would take to cover the leaf. Its bark provides an ideal environment for mosses, lichens, and ferns, giving a mature 100-foot-tall tree a disheveled look. In autumn, the maples' showy yellow leaves add brilliant color to the forest.

Where You Can Find Bigleaf Maple

Bigleaf maples grow best intermixed with evergreens. Look for them along streamsides

Bigleaf maple, Alan Leftridge

and around Lake Quinault, Sol Duc Hot Springs, and Hall of Mosses.

EPIPHYTES

Olympic's rain forests belong to the epiphytes—plants that get their moisture and nutrients from the rain and air. Although they are not parasitic, they usually grow on the backs of other plants. Walk the Hall of Mosses or Maple Glade Trails and you will see mosses, lichens, liverworts, club mosses, and licorice fern epiphytes crowding one another for light, water, and nutrients.

Moss-covered tree, Alan Leftridge

Sitka spruce, Alan Leftridge

Sitka Spruce
Picea sitchensis

Other common names include yellow spruce, tideland spruce, and coast spruce. The last two names tell where you can expect to find them growing. Olympic National Park has stands of Sitka spruce growing with western hemlock within 20 miles of the coast wherever moist maritime air and summer fogs maintain humid conditions. This is critical because Sitka spruce trees are not able to control water loss through their needles.

Where You Can Find Sitka Spruce

Look for Sitka spruce on the west side of Olympic National Park from the coastal plain to the seaward mountain slopes. The nation's largest Sitka spruce is near Quinault, off South Shore Road, in Olympic National Forest. It is a 0.3-mile walk to the giant.

Western Redcedar
Thuja plicata

Western redcedar trees grow best in moist, streamside soils, which are perfect for their shallow root systems. However, because they have no taproot to anchor them, they are vulnerable to winds. You will see western redcedar trees toppled along moist flats and streams. They can reach 200 feet under ideal growing conditions. Long, fibrous bark strands that hang from the trunks distinguish it from other trees in the coastal and lowland forests.

Where You Can Find Western Redcedar
Look for western redcedar along streams on the west side of the park. The largest western redcedar is along the Quinault Big Cedar Trail off the North Shore Road.

Western redcedar, Alan Leftridge

Alaska Cedar
Callitropsis nootkatensis

Alaska cedar is one of the slowest growing conifers in the park. Also known as yellow-cedar, some trees are over 3,500 years old. Found at sea level in British Columbia, they rarely grow below 2,000 feet in Olympic. In winter, the crown branches sag, shedding snow that cascades off lower branches, thereby protecting them from weight buildup.

Where You Can Find Alaska Cedar
Alaska cedar is a subalpine species in Olympic. You will find many specimens along Hurricane Ridge.

Alaska cedar, Nate Hough-Snee

Western hemlock, NPS photo

Western Hemlock
Tsuga heterophylla

Western hemlock, the state tree of Washington, is an understory tree that is genetically programmed to tolerate shade, so it thrives in the shadow of Douglas-firs and spruces. It can outlive the firs and spruces, and free of competition for sunlight, water, and nutrients, it can grow over 200 feet. The largest western hemlock in the United States is in Olympic National Park, with a height of more than 237 feet. On small hemlocks, dense branches grow close to the ground, providing winter cover for birds and mammals. Western hemlock lives at lower elevations than its cousin, the mountain hemlock.

Where You Can Find Western Hemlock
Look for western hemlock in any of the west-side valleys within the rain forest and lowland forest zones. The largest specimen is in the Quinault Valley.

KRUMMHOLZ FORMATIONS AND FLAG TREES

Krummholz (German for "crooked wood") is a miracle of subalpine forests. Exposure to the wind and cold causes trees to become stunted and contorted. Rock formations shelter the trees from the assault of driving snow and force them to grow in a tight group for survival. The protected areas of these trees continue to grow, causing them to become uniquely dense.

A variation on krummholz is a flag tree. Branches on the windward side are killed or deformed by icy winds that blast new growth, giving the tree a special flag-like appearance. The lower portion of the tree is often protected by snow and lacks the flagging. While krummholz trees grow in small groups, flagged trees often grow alone. In Olympic National Park, the species that form krummholz include subalpine fir and mountain hemlock. Hurricane Ridge is a good place to see both of these unusual natural wonders.

Douglas-fir

Pseudotsuga menziesii

Douglas-fir trees grow in every life zone in Olympic except the alpine. Near the coast, they can grow to more than 200 feet tall, but subalpine Douglas-firs are barely over 20 feet. Often referred to as Doug-fir, they are a favorite

Douglas-fir, NPS photo

of the building industry, with the wood used for house framing throughout the Northwest. Logging practices since the 1800s have favored clear-cutting practices, which are beneficial to Douglas-fir seedlings, as they thrive in sunlight. Doug-fir dominates most of the Pacific Northwest forests outside Olympic National Park. Within the park, western hemlock and western redcedar are the climax species.

Where You Can Find Douglas-fir

Douglas-fir groves are common in the lowland zone. The largest Douglas-fir is in the Olympic National Forest near Quinault. It is over 280 feet tall, with a circumference of more than 42 feet at the base.

WILDLIFE SKYSCRAPERS

Look for standing dead trees as you walk the trails and drive the roads. Known as snags (an old Scandinavian word for "stump of a tree"), these dead trees are critical to Olympic's ecology.

Snags are home to insects, provide nesting for birds and squirrels, and extend shelter to a myriad of animals during storms. The tallest snags provide the best animal shelter. These skyscraper environments limit predator access to roosting and nesting wildlife. Here is a list of ways that snags help wildlife:

- *Eagles, herons, ospreys, and hawks perch and nest on the tops of snags.*
- *Woodpeckers feed on insects living within.*
- *Bats roost and birds nest under overhanging loose bark.*
- *Woodpeckers, ducks, owls, and squirrels nest in snag cavities.*

Nationwide, 85 percent of all bird species use snags for nesting or shelter. Nutrients bound in snags begin recycling when wind and rot send them crashing to the ground. Snags that fall into creeks, marshes, and lakes help create spawning areas for fish, and habitat for aquatic insects that then become food for fish. Look around you . . . how many wildlife skyscrapers do you see?

Pacific silver fir, USBLM photo

Pacific Silver Fir
Abies amabilis

The botanical name *amabilis* is Latin for "lovely." Sometimes called white fir, the Pacific silver fir gets its name from its silvery color when seen from below. It is also identifiable by its smooth, ghost-gray bark splotched with white. This shade-tolerant tree is associated with western hemlock in Olympic. The oldest known Pacific silver fir is on Vancouver Island, British Columbia, at over 550 years old.

Where You Can Find Pacific Silver Fir
Pacific silver firs favor the montane zone, which you pass through on the drive to Hurricane Ridge. The largest specimen is in the Bogachiel Valley of Olympic National Park.

Mountain Hemlock
Tsuga mertensiana

Mountain hemlock is a subalpine tree in Olympic, associated with subalpine fir and Pacific silver fir. It thrives in areas of long winters with considerable snow. The seeds germinate on rotten logs, which provide nutritional support for the young trees that may live another 800 years. Mountain hemlock is deep-shade tolerant and grows into shrubby krummholz patches on cold, windy sites near the treeline.

Mountain hemlock, USDA photo

Where You Can Find Mountain Hemlock
Mountain hemlock can be found on Hurricane Ridge and at Deer Park. Several large examples grow in the upper reaches of the Quinault River Valley.

Lodgepole Pine
Pinus contorta

This tree gets its name because native people traditionally used its trunk to make the frames of their lodges. Today, the tree is also frequently used to build the shells of log homes. *Pinus contorta* means "contorted pine." The scientific name does not describe the straight and extended appearance of some of the lodgepole pine trees that you will see inland in the park. The botanists who first identified the characteristics of the lodgepole pine were studying specimens growing on the north coast. Salt air and the wind affect the lodgepole's growth patterns, causing the

Lodgepole pine, NPS photo

trees to grow twisted and stunted, hence the scientific name.

Where You Can Find Lodgepole Pine

You will see lodgepole pine trees in the montane and lowland forest zones. Lodgepole pine trees are also known as shore pines. The trees grow in their characteristic contorted manner in the coastal zone.

Subalpine Fir
Abies lasiocarpa

Subalpine firs are forest pioneers on disturbed sites. New trees assist in rehabilitating the landscape by protecting watershed soils. Subalpine firs can withstand Olympic National Park's coldest temperatures. Their steeple-like shape enables them to shake off heavy snow loads. The fallen snow presses lower branches to the ground where they root and perpetuate the krummholz growth pattern and provide excellent wildlife cover.

Where You Can Find Subalpine Fir

The easiest place to see subalpine fir in the park is on Hurricane Ridge, where the tree is abundant.

Subalpine fir, Alan Leftridge

NURSE LOGS AND OCTOPUS TREES

Olympic's rain forests are wet. Consequently, the cycle of cleansing fires spans hundreds of years. Without fires, the nutrient-rich forest floors are covered with several inches of dead leaves and tree needles, collectively known as litter. When fire does not clear the dead layers, the roots of germinating seeds cannot reach the soil, so the seedlings die. Decaying logs and stumps provide a rich substrate without an overlying litter layer. As you walk rain forest trails, you will see logs where trees have sprouted. They are known as nurse logs. Look for stumps with tree roots extending to the ground. They are called octopus trees.

Octopus tree, Alan Leftridge

BEST ACTIVITIES FOR CHILDREN

Olympic National Park is for everyone and is particularly inviting for children. Here are park activities that you can do with your children to increase their awareness, reveal wonders, and build lasting memories.

Learning about insects, NPS photo, Masyih Ford

Be a Junior Ranger

Explore, learn, and protect as a Junior Ranger! Children attend a ranger-led program and complete at least five activities in a Junior Ranger booklet. Olympic National Park Junior Ranger badges are awarded when a park ranger checks a child's booklet for completed activities. Junior Ranger materials are available for ages 5 and up. Get them at the Junior Ranger headquarters at the children's Discovery Room in the Olympic National Park Visitor Center. Your child can also participate online at the National Park Service's WebRangers site: www.nps.gov/webrangers/.

Go on a Photo Safari

Put that smartphone or digital camera to a good educational use. Help your kids organize their photos into a story about their vacation or day hike. Select a theme like "Patterns of Olympic National Park." Help your child to see and capture images of patterns, such as patterns in plant growth, types of flowers, tree leaves, where animals are found, lichen growth, clouds, weather, and people movement. Encourage them to post their story on their favorite social media site. Want a topic other than Patterns? Possibilities abound—Change, Adaptation, Interdependence, Similarities, Differences—or create your own theme.

Attend an Evening Program

Kids love attending evening programs. Help them learn about the fascinating diversity of Olympic National Park with an experienced park ranger. Topics include bears, birds, history, climate change, the night sky, and geology. Presentations are given at campgrounds. Check the park newspaper (the *Bugler*) for specific times and locations.

Join in a Ranger-led Hike

The National Park Service has ranger-led programs uniquely designed for youth and families. See the *Bugler*, distributed at entrance stations, and look for "Ranger Programs."

You will find child-centered programs at the Olympic National Park Visitor Center and the Hurricane Ridge Visitor Center.

Ranger and visitors, Alan Leftridge

Take a Walk in the Park

Do you want to explore the park with your child without a guide? Olympic National Park has more than 600 miles of trails. Start with short, educational, and exciting walks that will inspire your child to learn. Brochures for self-guided trails are available at the Olympic National Park Visitor Center in Port Angeles and at the trailheads.

Lake Crescent Area

Moments in Time Nature Trail, 0.5 mile round-trip, 30 minutes, no elevation gain. From the Storm King Ranger Station, this trail meanders through forest, meadows, and along the shore of Lake Crescent. Abundant and myriad flora and fauna line the path. The trail connects to the Marymere Falls Trail for an extended 2-mile adventure.

Elwah River Valley

Madison Falls Trail, 0.25 mile round-trip, 20 minutes, no elevation gain. This is a short walk through a cool forest to a lovely waterfall. Take time to admire the mammoth spruce trees near the road and read the interpretive sign at the south end of the parking lot.

Staircase Area

Staircase Rapids Nature Trail, 2 miles round-trip, 90 minutes, moderate elevation gain. Your child will delight in walking through an old-growth forest parallel to the Skokomish River's rushing waters. The trail ends at Staircase Rapids.

Would you like to take on more challenging experiences? Consider your child's abilities and choose some short unguided walks where you and your child can share in the discoveries of Olympic's myriad wonders. Make sure to bring snacks and water.

GOOD HIKES FOR KIDS

Lake Crescent Area

Marymere Falls Trail, 1.8 miles round-trip, 90 minutes, 80-foot elevation gain. Investigate a lowland forest, rushing creek, and a picturesque waterfall.

Sol Duc Area

Sol Duc Falls Trail, 1.6 miles round-trip, 60 minutes, no elevation gain. Trailside is loaded with interesting and varied understory growth. The waterfall is a must-see feature.

Hurricane Ridge Area

Meadow Loop Trail, 0.5-mile loop, 30 minutes, no elevation gain. The area teems with birds, marmots, deer, and great vistas.

Hoh Rain Forest Area

Hall of Mosses, 0.8 mile round-trip, 60 minutes, 100-foot elevation gain. This trail is the best and easiest way to introduce your child to the rain forest. Be sure to take the side trip to the maple grove.

Kalaloch Area

Ruby Beach, 0.5 mile round-trip, 30 minutes, no elevation gain. Children are attracted to rushing streams, waterfalls, and crashing surf. Ruby Beach is easily accessible and a great place to explore.

Read Aloud

Be prepared. A rainy day or a lull in activities gives you an opportunity to read a book with your child. Many entertaining and informative books are available at the Olympic National Park Visitor Center in Port Angeles. Pick some that you want to read and that will give your child a better understanding of Olympic National Park's heritage.

Heighten anticipation of the trip. Contact Discover Your Northwest at www.discovernw.org and order books that will delight your child. Read to them as you travel to Olympic. Here are some of the many available books that will enhance a child's experiences in the park:

- *Black Bear Babies* (ages 0 to 3)
- *How Do Bears Sleep?* E. J. Bird (ages 2 and up)
- *The Cutest Critter,* Marion Bauer and Stan Tekiela (ages 2 and up)
- *Lost in the Woods,* Carl R. Sams II and Jean Stoick (ages 2 and up)
- *Lil' MacDonald Likes to Hike,* Jennifer Taylor Tormalehto (ages 4 and up)
- *Who Pooped in the Park? Olympic National Park,* Gary Robson (ages 5 to 8)
- *A Child's Introduction to the Night Sky,* Michael Driscoll and Meredith Hamilton (ages 8 and up)
- *National Geographic Kids National Parks Guide U.S.A.,* National Geographic Kids (ages 8 and up)

Ride a Horse

Give your children a sense of what it must have been like to see Olympic National Park before automobiles became the primary source of transportation. Rides are 1 and 2 hours through the temperate rain forest. Outfitters adjacent to the park in Forks offer rides for ages 8 and older.

Horse pack train, NPS photo

Reflect

Today's fast-paced, gadget-filled lifestyle is busy with distractions. Olympic National Park presents wonderful opportunities to take a deep breath and reconnect with the natural world. Find a quiet, peaceful spot. Challenge your child to sit in solitude for 5 or 10 minutes. (Try it yourself!) Ask them to think about what they hear, smell, and see. Encourage them to write about or draw a picture about the experience and what their senses reveal to them. As they settle in for the night, ask your child to reflect on what they liked about the day's activities.

View the Night Sky

More than 80 percent of Americans live in cities and suburbs. Living in the glow of urban lights, children do not experience the excitement of seeing the Milky Way, August's Perseids meteor shower, or summer constellations. Olympic National Park's dark night skies are excellent for stargazing. Do it on your own or attend one of the Night Sky Programs, offered throughout the summer by park rangers. The park offers two programs: Hurricane Ridge Astronomy Program and Full Moon on Hurricane Hill. See the *Bugler* for dates, times, and information. The night sky inspires awe in a child, and its mysteries are brought to light when a family member takes the time to share in the discovery.

Milky Way, NPS photo, Neal Herbert

BEST THINGS TO DO ON A RAINY OR SNOWY DAY

Weather can be raw and dramatic on the coastline and on mountain ridges. That innocent cloud to the west can turn a warm sunny day into a cold rainy one in minutes. Accept the drama as a fact of visiting the wild Olympic. Make the most of unexpected weather with activities such as these:

Puddles, NPS photo

- Photograph the stormy conditions; they make some of the most interesting images.

- Park in a pullout and watch wildlife from your car. Stormy weather sends most humans indoors, but other animals carry on their outdoor lives.

- Bundle up and take a stroll around the Meadow Loop Trail on Hurricane Ridge.

- Spend extra time in the Olympic National Park Visitor Center in Port Angeles, and make sure that you see what's showing in the auditorium.

- Spend extra time at the Hurricane Ridge Visitor Center where you can shop, have a warm drink, and watch the weather through the large observation windows.

- Curl up with a book about Olympic in the lobby at Lake Crescent Lodge or Lake Quinault Lodge.

WINTER IN OLYMPIC

When autumn returns to Olympic, visitors are fewer. Cold North Pacific air rushes in while most backcountry travelers, day-hikers, campers, and sightseers withdraw. This is the beginning of a time of magic, a silent beauty not seen the rest of the year.

Although the spring and summer flowers are gone, the bigleaf maple leaves turn, adding brilliant yellow to the myriad green shades of the rain forest. U.S. Highway 101 is lined with yellowing ferns that soon become bronze. You will find the rain forest understory carpeted in these ferns.

Winter is a splendid time for a trip to Olympic, to experience how the rain forests, beaches, waterfalls, and mountains differ from summer. Great places to visit in winter are Rialto Beach, the Hoh Rain Forest, the waterfalls, and Hurricane Ridge.

Rialto Beach

Experience the thundering of giant waves crashing onshore. You may see huge trees tossed in the surf, having been washed down the rivers during rainstorms. Make sure that you check the tide chart and aim for low tide. Then you can explore the diversity of the tide pools. Rialto is one of the most photographed and striking beaches of Olympic. You can drive right to the beach and walk to the tide pools and see fascinating rock formations.

Hoh Rain Forest

Winter is the wet season and the forest drips with rain, showcasing its luxurious, healthy greens. The winter rains rejuvenate the myriad lichens, fungi, and mosses. Bright-colored mosses blanket the tree trunks and branches. Explore the 0.8-mile Hall of Mosses loop trail. Even if it is raining, it will be an experience that you will long remember.

The Waterfalls

Waterfalls are at their height of beauty during the rainy season. Three that are easy to access are Marymere Falls, Sol Duc Falls, and Madison Falls. There is a high probability that it will rain during your visit, so expect the trails to be muddy.

Marymere Falls

The trail winds through an old-growth lowland forest. Marymere is a spectacular waterfall any time of year, but extraordinary when it is frozen.

Sol Duc Falls

The trail is cut through an old-growth forest. Look for elk that often linger here during winter. The falls are large, loud, and dramatic with the season's heavy water flow.

Madison Falls

Madison is the easiest waterfall to view. It is a mere 500 feet from the parking lot. This is a good stop for small children to enjoy.

Hurricane Ridge

The ridge can be sparkling sunny in the winter, even when it is raining at Port Angeles. The park service plows the road, but conditions can be slick; all vehicles are required to carry tire chains from November through March. In winter, the road is open Friday, Saturday, and Sunday and closed weekdays, except between Christmas and New Year's, when it's open daily. Weather permitting, walk up Hurricane Hill for the inspiring panorama.

Snowshoeing on Hurricane Ridge, NPS photo

Hurricane Ridge Ski and Snowboard Area

Because Hurricane Ridge is a popular destination for snowshoeing, tubing, and cross-country skiing, the park service grants a lease for a small, family-owned ski area. This gives visitors the additional opportunity to enjoy snowboarding and downhill skiing. The ski area operates from mid-December to March.

You will find many worthwhile winter activities in Olympic National Park. Just make sure to check the weather forecasts and tide charts, and come prepared for snow or rain.

BEST BOOKS ABOUT OLYMPIC NATIONAL PARK

Enrich your adventure by reading a book about Olympic National Park. Read before arrival and bring other books along just in case it rains. Here are some books and travel guides that you can find at your local bookstore or through Discover Your Northwest, www.discovernw.org.

- *Olympic National Park Impressions*, 2003, James Randklev.
- *Barrier Free Travel: For Wheelers and Slow Walkers*, 2015, Candy Harrington.
- *The Last Wilderness*, 1976, Murray Morgan.
- *Olympic Battleground: Creating and Defending Olympic National Park*, 2000, Carsten Lien.
- *Gods & Goblins: A Field Guide to Place Names of Olympic National Park*, 2009, Smitty Parrett.
- *Across the Olympic Mountains: The Press Expedition, 1889-90*, 1989, Robert Wood.
- *Women to Reckon With: Untamed Women of the Olympic Wilderness*, 2007, Gary Peterson and Glynda Schaad.
- *The Definitive Guide: Olympic National Park and Peninsula*, 2015, Douglas Scott.
- *A Quick Field Guide to Tidepools of the Pacific Coast*, 2008, Michael Rigby.
- *Olympic Mountains Trail Guide*, 2000, Robert L. Wood.
- *Top Trails: Olympic National Park and Vicinity*, 2014, Douglas Lorain.
- *Best Easy Day Hikes: Olympic National Park*, 2015, Eric Molvar.
- *Native Peoples of the Olympic Peninsula: Who We Are*, 2003, Jacilee Wray.
- *Birds of Washington Field Guide*, 2001, Stan Tekiela.
- *Mushrooms of Northwest North America*, 1994, Helene Schalkwijk-Barendsen.

GREAT SUBJECTS TO PHOTOGRAPH

Hoh entrance sign, Alan Leftridge

Olympic is a huge national park. Ninety-five percent of the land area is wilderness. The center of the park is dominated by the Olympic Mountains, penetrable only on foot. You must travel by vehicle to see the easiest-to-reach features. Driving from one side of the park to the other side takes more than 4 hours. If this is your first trip to Olympic National Park, you likely will be taking pictures of everything that attracts your interest.

Here are some of the emblematic landscape features and objects that you can expect to photograph on a one- or two-day visit.

- An Olympic National Park entrance sign
- Any Olympic National Park visitor center
- Olympic Mountains from Hurricane Ridge Visitor Center
- Strait of Juan de Fuca from Hurricane Ridge Meadow Loop Trail
- Wildlife along Hurricane Hill Trail
- Hurricane Ridge Visitor Center
- Lake Crescent Lodge
- Lake Crescent from any of the turnouts along the south shore
- Sunset from Lake Crescent
- Marymere Falls
- Soc Duc Falls

- Avalanche lilies
- Olympic Roosevelt elk
- Black-tailed deer

The following are some of the iconic features that you can reach to photograph on a three- or four-day visit.

- Lake Quinault
- Lake Quinault Lodge
- Rain gauge at Lake Quinault Lodge
- Quinault Rain Forest
- Hall of Mosses in Hoh Rain Forest
- Olympic Roosevelt elk
- Point of the Arches
- Sunset from any of the beaches
- Ruby Beach
- Kalaloch Beach
- Rialto Beach
- La Push Beaches (First, Second, and Third)

The best times to photograph these features are before 10 a.m. and after 4 p.m. in order to avoid deep contrasting shadows. Many professional photographers look for clear skies the morning following a cold front. Don't hide from stormy weather—the clouds can provide dramatic lighting.

Rain gauge, Lake Quinault Lodge, Alan Leftridge

BEST PLACES TO TAKE A GROUP PORTRAIT

Record your visit to Olympic for posterity: take a group portrait. Most visitors look for the most memorable and iconic locations for picture backdrops. Popular spots include:

- Any of the park entrance signs
- Along the Hall of Mosses Nature Trail
- The back patio of the Hurricane Ridge Visitor Center
- Along the Meadow Loop Trail at Hurricane Ridge
- The turnout at 9.4 miles on Hurricane Ridge Road that faces toward the Strait of Juan de Fuca
- Rialto Beach with humongous driftwood
- Ruby Beach with sea stacks in the backdrop
- The gazebo at Kalaloch Lodge overlooking Kalaloch Beach

Say cheese!, Alan Leftridge

BEST SCENIC VIEWS

Olympic's best scenic views are in the high country, at the coastline, and along lakefronts where you can enjoy broad panoramas. Here are some suggestions for seeing the depth and breadth of the vastness of Olympic National Park.

Hurricane Ridge, Alan Leftridge

Hurricane Ridge
This is the best vista in the park to view the mountains that reign over the wilds of Olympic. You can circumnavigate the park on U.S. Highway 101 and not get a better sighting of Mount Olympus than at the Hurricane Ridge Visitor Center.

Hurricane Ridge Meadow Loop
From the parking lot atop Hurricane Ridge, the paved Meadow Loop Trail provides wide-angle views of Port Angeles, the Strait of Juan de Fuca, Vancouver Island, the San Juan Islands, and the Bailey Range.

Obstruction Point
After traveling at least 4 miles on this unpaved road, you will be rewarded with multiple scenic views of Mount Olympus and the Bailey Range. Early summer is best for mountain range photographs with wildflowers in the foreground. Obstruction Point is 8 miles from Hurricane Ridge, and offers splendid panoramic views.

The road is gravel, steep, and winding. Recommended for passenger cars only.

Ruby Beach
Ruby is a picturesque beach with various size sea stacks offshore.

Olympic coast, Jenny Baker

Onshore, the beach features lovely polished colorful rocks, a stream, lots of driftwood, and a coastal forest rising above cliffs. Wander the beach observing patterns in the rocks, wood, and tide pools.

Rialto Beach

Rialto Beach is renowned for its many sea stacks, rock formations, and gargantuan driftwood trees littering the beach. The area also abounds in wildlife. Take a walk about 1.5 miles north to Hole-in-the-Wall. If timing of the tides allows, stay for sunset.

Lake Crescent

Several pullouts along U.S. Highway 101 offer splendid views of Lake Crescent. Quieter viewpoints include the shore in front of Lake Crescent Lodge, East Beach Picnic Area off East Beach Road, and Fairholme.

Lake Crescent, Alan Leftridge

BEST SUNRISE AND SUNSET SPOTS

Lake Crescent, NPS photo, Jon Preston

While touring Olympic National Park in the early morning or late afternoon, you may chance upon patterns of constantly changing colors in the eastern or western sky. Multihued sunrises and sunsets frame the landscape, provoking awe and reflection. Here are some places with memorable views at dawn and day's end.

Sunrise

The best sunrise views are from unobstructed vistas, such as mountain peaks. But all require that you begin your hike well before dawn to reach your destination. Here are some places where walking is minimal from a parking lot.

- Hurricane Ridge
- Fairholme, at the west end of Lake Crescent
- Log Cabin Resort

Sunset

The best sunset views are from the beaches. Consider:

- Ruby Beach
- La Push Beaches (First, Second, or Third)
- Kalaloch Beach
- Rialto Beach
- Shi Shi Beach

Not close to a beach? Try:

- Lake Crescent Lodge
- Sledgehammer Point, Lake Crescent
- East Beach Picnic Area, Lake Crescent
- Lake Quinault Lodge

Get both sunrise and sunset on the same day at the top of Blue Mountain by way of the 0.5-mile loop Rain Shadow Nature Trail at the end of Deer Park Road.

RESOURCES

Reading the *Bugler*, NPS photo, D. Archuleta

There are many chances for you to learn about the natural and cultural heritage of Olympic National Park. The National Park Service and private foundations offer many opportunities that will enhance your visit.

General Park Information
Olympic National Park
600 East Park Avenue
Port Angeles, Washington 98362
Email: olym_visitor_center@nps.gov
360.565.3131 for current road, campground, and weather information

Wilderness Information Center and Backcountry Permit Office (WIC)
360.565.3100

Hoh Rainforest Visitor Center
360.374.6925

Quinault Wilderness Information Office
360.288.0232

Discover Your Northwest
www.discovernw.org
360.565.3195

Discover Your Northwest is a nonprofit association that provides educational resources at park stores. Income subsidizes Olympic's programs, exhibits, and publications.

Friends of Olympic National Park
www.friendsonp.org
The Friends' group assists with park projects and advances understanding of Olympic's ecological, educational, economic, and recreational importance.

Nature Bridge
www.naturebridge.org/olympic-national-park
360.928.3720
Nature Bridge is a private, nonprofit educational organization located on the shores of Lake Crescent. Field science courses are offered for students.

Washington's National Park Fund
1904 Third Avenue, Suite 400
Seattle, Washington 98101
www.wnpf.org
206.623.2063
Washington's National Park Fund is a nonprofit group whose undertaking is to strengthen and protect national parks in Washington. The Fund advances volunteer and stewardship programs, and helps fund research and trail maintenance.

North Coast & Cascades Network
Jerry Freilich, PhD, Director
NCCN Science Learning Network
Email: jerry_freilich@nps.gov
www.nwparkscience.org/parks/olym
The North Coast & Cascades Network is one of 15 nationwide Research Learning Centers in the Science Learning Network. The mission of the network is to integrate research and education, and promote resource stewardship. The group supports, facilitates, promotes, and communicates through a virtual website.

Misty mountains, NPS photo, Dave Turner

ABOUT THE AUTHOR

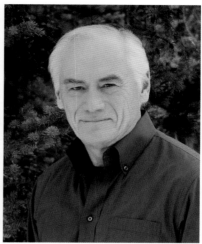

Alan Leftridge lived on the North Coast for over 25 years, teaching environmental studies at Humboldt State University. His experiences as a seasonal naturalist for the National Park Service, wilderness ranger, and executive editor of The Interpreter and Legacy magazines enhanced his exploration of the rich diversity of the region. The Best of Olympic National Park combines his knowledge of the geography, plants, animals, and sea life and his passion for teaching for the visitor who wants a memorable experience at Olympic National Park.

Alan earned a BS in biology at the University of Central Missouri, a secondary teaching credential from the University of Montana, and a PhD in science education at Kansas State University. His books include The Best of Rocky Mountain National Park, The Best of Yellowstone National Park, The Best of Glacier National Park, Glacier Day Hikes, Seeley-Swan Day Hikes, Going to Glacier, and Interpretive Writing.

Sea urchin, NPS photo, Bill Baccus